READING SKILLS

Improving Speed and Comprehension

W9-AXI-382

THIRD EDITION

WILLIAM D. BAKER

Wright State University
Dayton, Ohio

PRENTICE HALL, *Englewood Cliffs, New Jersey* 07632

LIBRARY OF CONGRESS
Library of Congress Cataloging-in-Publication Data

Baker, William D.
   Reading skills : improving speed and comprehension / William D.
Baker. -- 3rd ed.
      p.   cm.
   ISBN 0-13-762402-6
   1. Reading (Higher education)   I. Title.
LB2395.3.B34 1989
428.4'07'11--dc19   88-22675
                                                        CIP

Editorial/production supervision and
   interior design: Lisa A. Domínguez
Cover design: Zak Design
Manufacturing buyer: Ray Keating

© 1989 by Prentice-Hall, Inc.
A Division of Simon & Schuster
Englewood Cliffs, New Jersey 07632

Printed in the United States of America

10 9 8 7 6 5 4 3 2 1

ISBN   0-13-762402-6

Prentice-Hall International (UK) Limited, *London*
Prentice-Hall of Australia Pty. Limited, *Sydney*
Prentice-Hall Canada Inc., *Toronto*
Prentice-Hall Hispanoamericana, S.A., *Mexico*
Prentice-Hall of India Private Limited, *New Delhi*
Prentice-Hall of Japan, Inc., *Tokyo*
Simon & Schuster Asia Pte. Ltd., *Singapore*
Editora Prentice-Hall do Brasil, Ltda., *Rio de Janeiro*

Contents

Preface to the Third Edition

Almost a half-million copies of *Reading Skills* have been sold since the first edition was published in 1953. Since very few textbooks of any kind published in the early fifties are still around today, why does this book endure? I suspect that it keeps bubbling along because it works and because its methods are timeless.

And still the demand for the book continues. And why not? Staying on top of expanding knowledge and an avalanche of information is a challenge. Although *Reading Skills* does not guarantee success, it will point the way.

How many books do you read each year? Would you like to read more books and get more out of them? If so, you have come to the right place.

How rapidly are you reading now? Fifty words a minute? Three hundred? Five hundred? If you are not sure, time yourself on one of the measured chapter readings, using the Time-Rate Table at the back of the book to find your rate. If you practice conscientiously and follow the suggestions in the remaining chapters, there is nothing to stop you from reading anything twice as fast as you do now. Faster reading will give you more pleasure, more knowledge, and a richer life.

For more than three decades people have been able to double their rate of reading by working through this book. You can do it too, and when you do, you will reap the benefits for the rest of your days.

In the third edition I have deliberately shunned such utilitarian selections as "How to Bake a Meringue Pie," assuming that good reading ranges far beyond formulas and lists. Indeed, if a text such as this can be said to have a tone that distinguishes it from others, one could call the tone here humanistic. An indication of that tone is shown by the authors chosen to illustrate (or demonstrate) points in the text: Sherwood Anderson, Aristotle, Sir Francis Bacon, Pearl Buck, Thomas Carlyle, Willa Cather, Kate Chopin, Charles Darwin, Charles Dickens, Emily Dickinson, John Donne, Ralph Waldo Emerson, Abraham Flexner, Benjamin Franklin, Sigmund Freud, Edith Hamilton, Nathaniel Hawthorne, Ernest Hemingway, Homer, Aldous Huxley, Henrik Ibsen, Henry James, William James, Sinclair Lewis, Abraham Lincoln, John Locke, James Russell Lowell, Herman Melville, Arthur Miller, John Milton, Toni Morrison, Michel Montaigne, Flannery O'Connor, Tillie Olsen, George Orwell, Plato, Edgar Allan Poe, Katherine Anne Porter, Marcel Proust, John Ruskin, Helen Santmyer, J. D. Salinger, William Saroyan, William Shakespeare, Percy Bysshe Shelley, Gertrude Stein, Harriet Beecher Stowe, Henry David Thoreau, Leo Tolstoy, Mark Twain, Alice Walker, H.G. Wells, Eudora Welty, Edith Wharton, Thomas Wolfe, Virginia Woolf, and Richard Wright.

For the most part this is an eclectic book, one that culls what seem to me the best ideas and reading techniques from a large number of reading manuals and books on reading. I wish to acknowledge my indebtedness to authors who have trod this ground before me. I also am under obligation to those who have used the book and have offered constructive criticism.

I wish to thank the following for permission to reproduce material in this book: Harper & Brothers for the extract from Abraham Flexner, "The Usefulness of Useless Knowledge," Harper's Magazine, used by permission of Harper & Brothers; the American Library Association for the Library Bill of Rights; and the *American Heritage Dictionary.*

William D. Baker

How to Use Reading Skills

Chapters 1 through 16 of this book offer information on how to increase your reading efficiency. In conducting reading services and college English classes, I have found that almost everyone who has read this has achieved a reading rate of 400 words per minute or better. The average reader starts at about 270 and finishes at about 525 words per minute. One woman read the last chapter at 2400 words per minute and had excellent comprehension of the material.

I should like to emphasize here that extremely rapid rates are possible only for relatively easy material, for which this book was deliberately designed. Although I have written with average readers in mind, I have reduced to a minimum the factors (high-powered vocabulary and long and involved sentence structure) that make reading difficult. If you hope to make the track team, it is best to increase your running efficiency on smooth, level ground. Similarly, it is best to increase your reading efficiency on material of standard, or a little below standard, difficulty—the level, say, of popular magazines. Occasionally the application exercises include passages of a higher level of difficulty, to emphasize the importance of reading different levels of material in different ways. Not everything *can* be read at the same rate of speed and not everything in this book *should* be read at the same rate of speed. However, you should apply what you know about reading skills to even the most difficult materials.

Chapters 17 to 24 deal with important reading skills that are often neglected. In developmental reading programs it is not unusual for the work to stop with a consideration of the basic reading skills discussed in the first sixteen chapters. This is unfortunate, because these basic skills, important as they are, are just the beginning. You should advance beyond the utilitarian, textbook type of reading into the excitement of literature and other reading for enjoyment. The early chapters suggest means of chewing and digesting your everyday reading on the job or in the classroom, while the later ones are concerned with improving your literary appetite and developing a taste for good reading.

When All Else Fails, Read the Directions

An important feature of this book is that each chapter can be read for two purposes: *to learn how to become a better reader* and *to develop speed*. To get the most out of this book, you should try to read one chapter a day or, at the very least, three a week, as fast as you can. Application

Exercises—revised in the third edition—enable you to practice the principles of skillful reading that each chapter sets forth. In addition, you will find questions that test your comprehension of what you have just read in the chapter-by-chapter Comprehension Checks beginning on page 110. The answers are provided on page 136 so you can immediately check your accuracy of understanding.

Here is the way to use each chapter: *Begin timing your reading directly after the chapter title*, reading as fast as you can. Do not forget that comprehension is just as important as speed.

When you finish the selection, record the length of time it has taken in minutes and seconds. Use the Time-Rate Table (on page 138) to convert this time into your reading rate for that selection. Record your rate in the space provided at the end of the selection. For example, if you take five minutes to read Chapter 1, a check in the rate table will show your reading rate to be 250 words per minute.

Immediately after recording your rate for each selection, you should turn to the Comprehension Check for that chapter in the last part of the book and answer the questions carefully—without looking back over the chapter. You should always answer a good percentage correctly, and if you miss more than three, you should not count your rate score for that day.

Record your rate and comprehension scores on the Graph of Progress at the back of the book. When you have done so, begin work on the Application Exercise for that chapter. In order to make the book more useful to you, you should work on these various materials such as practice exercises, recall devices, vocabulary quizzes, and suggestions for further study that have been placed after each chapter. Their purpose is to allow you to apply what you learned to a practical reading situation. Most of them allow careful and unhurried reading and call for you to read with pencil in hand. Answer keys, when needed, appear at the end of the chapter or on a specified page.

A careful working of the application exercises and vocabulary checks will help improve your reading rate even though they are usually untimed exercises. Why? The more seriously you attack *all* aspects of your reading, the more effort you will automatically give to improving your rate. In other words, your rate increases in proportion to the effort you make to increase it. It's as simple as that.

1 *Keeping Up with the Stream*

Events stream past our minds like jet streams, and if we want to be well informed we need to do more than stand and gawk at the vapor scratches in the sky after the jet has passed. We need to be there when it happens. Significant social, economic, and political issues, all demanding serious and open-minded investigation, more than ever before require a high level of reader enlightenment.

To advance in knowledge one must forever learn more, study more, reason more. Reading helps accomplish this; in college about 85 percent of all study involves reading—especially in a computer age. If, as it certainly does, progress comes through study, then reading is the chief means to academic progress.

Since reading is so vitally significant, all of us need to take a close look at our reading habits. The ability to read and the ability to choose good reading material characterize people just as much as do their appearance and speech. Our reading habits are as much a part of us as our ability to hold our own in a discussion or our ability to judge the difference between people. The way we read is closely connected with the way we think.

Check your reading habits by searching your mind for the answers to these questions: Do you read as well as you can? When you read fast, do you understand what you read? Are your reading habits based on sound principles? Do you know what sound principles of reading are? Can you read to make judgments about the relationship between a presentation of the facts and the truth? Are you skillful at determining the meaning of words as they appear in context? Are you an efficient reader?

What are efficient readers? They are people who can race through an ordinary novel very rapidly. Their eyes move quickly over the lines of print, and their accuracy of comprehension is high. They grasp what they read, and they retain for a long period what they have read. They know that it is important to read different materials differently. They first skim a book that they intend to read thoroughly. They always read for a purpose, whether that purpose be sheer pleasure, information, or a combination of the two. They take notes, mental or otherwise, on technical information or on difficult material. And of utmost importance, they concentrate intensively when they read. Reading brings to them some of their keenest pleasures in life; they experience a real satisfaction in doing a thing well. The more they read the better readers they become, because in practicing correct habits, they become more skillful readers.

You probably believe that it is possible to read faster than you do now, but there is probably also a persistent doubt in the back of your mind that your understanding will keep pace. Get rid of that doubt, for it is that doubt rather than anything in the reading process itself that is slowing you down. You will understand just as much and in many cases more when you begin to read more rapidly. When you read rapidly, you will focus on whole thoughts and whole phrases instead of plodding along word by word at a snail's pace. Word-by-word reading yields little meaning; it is only when words are understood in relation to the other words in the phrase or sentence that they make sense. When you understand and accept this fact, you have taken one of the first important steps toward becoming a more efficient reader.

There are specific skills you must develop and practice to become more efficient. You should, for example, always seek to identify the main idea of whatever material you are reading. To illustrate: The main idea of this chapter is skillful reading, so you should remember the idea every time you start a new paragraph. You should say to yourself, "What does this paragraph say about skillful reading? What new information will be offered here? And how will this paragraph be related to the preceding one?" As you read along, you should observe and remember the important details and relate them to the main idea or to significant subordinate ideas. Further, you should also begin drawing a conclusion on the basis of the facts you read. Check to see what the facts are actually pointing out and whether these facts make sense to you. To do this, of course, you need to understand whether authors are explaining or are "secretly" persuading you to accept their point of view. Finally, you should relate what you have read to what you already know about the subject or to what you know about related subjects. If you do not relate what you read to the background of knowledge you now possess, you are reading in a vacuum.

Skillful reading is really an art in the sense that the more diligently you practice, the more proficient you will become.

After finishing the elementary grades, most of us never again have a formal reading lesson. Yet the ability to learn, an obviously important aspect of developing reading skill, increases with maturity. The fact, therefore, that you are now a slow reader does not mean that you must remain one. If you possess a strong and determined will to do so, *you can improve*. If you are now a good reader, you can become a better reader.

There is no royal road to skillful reading. But there are no insurmountable obstacles to it either. The relationship between your belief that you can improve and the actual improvement you make is very close. Success comes to believers.

Begin immediately. Read through each chapter in this book as fast as you can. Don't make the mistake of sacrificing meaning, however, just to get a faster reading rate. No matter what you're reading, comprehension is more important that speed. Yet you want to try to overcome slow habits as soon as you can. To do that, you have to settle down to try hard. Make a strong effort from the very beginning to read more rapidly and more skillfully.

Average rate for Chapter 1: 270 wpm. Turn to the Comprehension Check on page 110.

Application Exercise: Chapter 1

Get the Idea?

To apply what was stressed in Chapter 1, locate the main idea of the following paragraphs.

(Note: Getting the idea depends on understanding the vocabulary. Certain words are underlined in the following exercises; these words will appear in a vocabulary check on page 20.)

New Art Forms

Since World War II, various art forms have been altering and expanding our consciousness of what is; at the same time they are expanding the dimensions of art itself. If we consider the theater of the absurd, for example, we see conventional realism rejected as well as linear sequence. We see reality pictured as an illusion; we see that for the creators of this art, none of the old conventions exist. Thus, many of the practitioners of fiction feel that the true enemies of story form are the very things that made us understand the conventions of story form in the beginning: plot, characters, setting, and theme. So say the innovators, while we, as readers, are hanging on by our fingernails.

Write *B* in front of the statement if it is too broad an expression of the main idea; write *N* in front of the statement if it is too narrow an expression of the main idea; write *X* in front of the statement if it is a correct expression of the main idea.

_____ 1. Innovation in art often shows disrespect for old forms.
_____ 2. Innovators, using new forms and discarding the old, expand the public consciousness but may also confuse the public.
_____ 3. Without innovation art cannot be vital and in tune with the times.

Thoreau Asks for the Best Readers (*Walden*, 1854)

The best books are not read even by those who are called good readers. What does our Concord culture amount to? There is in this town, with very few exceptions, no taste for the best or for very good books even in English literature, whose words all can read and spell. Even the college-bred and so called liberally educated men here and elsewhere have really little or no acquaintance with the English classics; and as for the recorded wisdom of mankind, the ancient classics and

Bibles, which are <u>accessible</u> to all who will know of them, there are the feeblest efforts any where made to become acquainted with them.

Write B in front of the statement if it is too broad, N if it is too narrow, and X if it is a correct expression of the main idea.

_____ 1. Even college-bred people make feeble efforts to read the best books.
_____ 2. The rest of the country, like Concord, should read more good books.
_____ 3. The Bible and ancient and English classics should be read by all.

Thoreau and Uncommon Schools (*Walden,* 1854)

We boast that we belong to the nineteenth century and are making the most rapid strides of any nation. But consider how little this village does for its own culture. I do not wish to flatter my townsmen, nor to be flattered by them, for that will not advance either of us. We need to be <u>provoked</u>—<u>goaded</u> like oxen, as we are, into a trot. We have a comparatively decent system of common schools, schools for infants only; but excepting the half-starved [lecture hall] in the winter, and <u>latterly</u> the <u>puny</u> beginning of a library suggested by the state, no school for ourselves. We spend more on almost any article of bodily . . . <u>ailment</u> than on our mental [ailment.] It is time that we had uncommon schools, that we did not leave off our education when we begin to be men and women.

Write B in front of the statement if it is too broad, N if it is too narrow, and X if it is a correct expression of the main idea.

_____ 1. We spend more on medicine for our bodies than for our minds.
_____ 2. We should not boast about our culture but try to improve it by developing uncommon schools for men and women.
_____ 3. People should not stop learning after they leave common schools.

(1) N,X,B; (2) X,B,N; (3) N,X,B

2 *Figuring Out Your Rate*

Suppose when you went to the doctor with an irritating twinge in your right thigh, you were not examined but only given an aspirin and sent away. You would think, I am sure, that the doctor was very unprofessional, a person you would distrust for not taking the time to make a careful and thorough diagnosis. You would think the doctor a faker for treating you without giving thought to the proper cure.

Before you begin a reading program for yourself, you should make a careful survey of your reading habits. Analyze yourself by using a guide like the checklist at the end of this chapter or, better yet, by consulting a reading specialist. Only after such an analysis will you or anyone else know what to do to make you a better reader.

It is difficult to say what aspect of your reading habits you should consider first, because these habits are conditioned by your eyesight and general health, by your mental quickness, and by personality factors affecting your attitude. For example, your vision is important. If you have not recently had your eyes checked professionally, you should do so before you begin an intensive reading program. Such a program should not cause undue strain on your eyes, and if it teaches you to use your eyes more efficiently, it should in fact lessen the strain on them. Your reading can be seriously hampered, however, if you attempt to do a considerable amount of reading with faulty vision.

Perhaps, as speed is the particular reading skill that most people want above all others, you should first test your speed of reading. Use the chapters of this book to do this. Each chapter is 1000 words long, give or take a few words. Simply divide into 1000 the number of minutes it takes you to read each chapter. The result will be your reading speed in words per minute. The time-rate table in the back of the book does all the arithmetic for you.

What is the meaning of your rate as you work it out? If you are reading under 200 words per minute, the chances are that you are a word-by-word reader. You may find your lips moving, which means that you can read no faster than you can make your lips move. You will be harnessed to the speed of your lips until you can break that habit. If you thrust a pencil between your teeth or stick a knuckle in your mouth, you will find it almost impossible to lip-read.

If you read between 200 and 250 words per minute, you probably vocalize when you read. That is, you form each word in your throat as you see it on the printed page. This is also a very bad habit because it harnesses you to a slow speed. To discover whether or not you vocalize, place your fingertips on your throat in an attempt to feel vibrations as you read. Reading faster will control if not eliminate vocalizing.

Suppose you are reading at 300 words per minute or faster. That means you are a little faster than an average reader, but it doesn't mean this program is not for you. It probably means you will be able to improve your rate of reading even more than the average person.

Having surveyed your speed of reading, you must check other important aspects of your reading ability. One of these is vocabulary. Have you stumbled on some of the words of this chapter or not? A great deal of one's reading difficulty may be due to a limited vocabulary, which is something you can easily improve by persistent drill, discipline, and practice. When you puzzle out the meaning of a word, you obviously slow to a crawl. Perhaps knowing the meaning of words is not your difficulty. It may be that your "word attack" is not as good as it might be. Word attack refers to your ability to recognize the form of a word and its pronunciation. Many people, once they recognize a word, either know or can puzzle out its meaning. Their difficulty usually comes in recognition. If they knew how to attack the word, if they knew how to pronounce it, they would recognize it immediately and have no trouble with it. Learning how to pronounce words by learning vowel sounds, combined vowel sounds, and consonant-vowel sounds may be what you need to improve your reading efficiency.

Check your comprehension too. Read an article from a magazine you are familiar with, perhaps a hobby magazine, and then make a brief summary of it. Then bring up the subject matter in conversation with a friend, making an attempt to reveal more than a superficial knowledge of dates or statistics. Reveal, if you can, the implications of the statistics or the significance of the dates. Your object is to test your own understanding.

Comprehension is a process of organizing and memory, but it is more than mere recall; a grade-school pupil who has memorized Lincoln's Gettysburg Address may have very little conception of its meaning. Comprehension means understanding, and understanding *can* be improved, for it is not an inborn quality.

Good comprehension depends for the most part on your alertness and your ability to concentrate. If you can concentrate well, you can comprehend well, but if you are a daydreamer, reading will merely be an eye exercise for you.

Reading tests developed by universities and educational agencies have been given to thousands of students to determine their reliability and validity. These tests survey your speed of reading, your accuracy and level of comprehension, and your vocabulary. You can make a better diagnosis of your ability if you take a test like one of these instead of depending on your own estimate.

Finally, remember that you cannot improve your reading merely by wishing or by daydreaming. The first thing to do is to discover your reading weaknesses. Then make an intelligent effort to improve your reading habits. You are engaging on a self-improvement program that will make you a more skillful reader—*if you work at it.*

Record your rate here: _____

Average rate for Chapter 2: 295 wpm. Turn to the Comprehension Check on page 111.

Application Exercise: Chapter 2

Finding the Time

An important part of surveying your reading habits is making your weekly schedule. Are you making the best use of your time? Have you managed to find time for relaxing? for exercise? for getting to and from work? Is the schedule realistic?

The schedule you make should be custom designed for your own idiosyncrasies. It should be a plan, not a straightjacket. The details of scheduling are less significant than your intent to make effective use of your time.

Guidelines for Preparing a Weekly Schedule:

1. Make a grid plan like a blank calendar that allows for every waking hour of every day of the week, including weekends.
2. Enter on the grid plan all of your regular appointments: classes; labs; workshops; clinics; trips to the doctor, the grocery store, and the recycling center; doing the laundry.
3. Next enter your employment times.
4. Allow time for meals.
5. Enter times for study of *Reading Skills* and, if appropriate, other study material. It is best to regularize your schedule so your periods of study come at set times each week.
6. Allow time for physical recreation daily, even if it is only a walk or bike ride to discover the appearance of the day's world, or a short gardening session.
7. Allow time for mental recreation and enrichment. It might be watching television or a movie, chatting with friends, reading, listening to music, or reflection and contemplation.
8. After your schedule is made, look on it as a common-sense guide to your week. It need not be a rigid formula. Special projects and emergencies will always intrude.

Answer the following questions after you have prepared your weekly schedule. Then revise it, if necessary, in the light of your analysis.

1. If your schedule is for a typical week, is it sufficiently flexible to allow for occasional emergencies? (When do you make up for "lost" time?)
2. Did you include a fixed time for recreational reading? A time for a visit to the library?
3. Will your plan allow you to keep your free hours really free for spontaneous activity? (Isn't the feeling of freedom one has on a vacation one of the major reasons for deliberately scheduling "free" time?)
4. Is your schedule simple enough to allow you to live with it? (Is it true that guilty consciences come from schedules laboriously made and quietly abandoned?)
5. Does your schedule allow you "reward" time? (Is a relaxing hour before dinner your reward for a day of conscientious work?)

3 *Shaping Up*

An athlete who expects to move at top speed is very careful to keep in excellent physical condition, staying trim and cautiously observing the training rules. Similarly, if you expect to do the best job you can in reading, you should condition yourself to do it. You cannot expect to speed over the lines of print with tired or strained eyes. Here are some simple rules for keeping in good physical shape for skillful reading.

You should have your eyes checked regularly, once a year or so. Because your eyes are irreplaceable, you ought to give them the best possible care. If you wear glasses and have them checked from time to time, you need not worry about straining your eyes by reading excessively and at very rapid rates. Imperfect vision that has been corrected by glasses is perfectly satisfactory for reading and will not hold you back in any way. If you have been advised to wear glasses while reading, be sure to do so. When you begin to establish the reading habits of a skillful reader, you will begin to find real pleasure in the physical act of reading.

Good lighting is important in reading. The light should come from behind or at least be so placed that it is shielded from your eyes. It should be strong enough to light the page clearly and yet not so strong that it produces a glare. Too strong a light, such as direct sunlight, or bright fluorescent lighting, puts the worst kind of strain on your eyes and tires them. With ample, clear, and well-placed illumination, you will find that you can read for hours without tiring.

The page you are reading should be fourteen to sixteen inches from your eyes, but you may find it more comfortable to read at a little shorter or a little longer distance. Choose the distance that seems most natural and most comfortable for you. It is best to hold a book in your hands or to rest it in an inclined position when you read. Avoid reading for long periods of time from a book that is flat on a desk or table. Not only does it cause eye fatigue, but it also makes you hold your head in a strained position.

Some people have headaches and a strained or twitching feeling about the eyes after reading a long time. Most of them could avoid this unnecessary and dangerous discomfort if from time to time they would look away from the book and rest their eyes on some distant object. Your eyes are wonderful mechanical devices, but they need your considerate treatment if they are to continue to function well. In their movements over the printed page they use up almost as much energy in a few minutes as they would in dwelling on a distant landscape for a much longer period. If you plan to spend the whole evening reading, take a short break every half hour or so. Now and then look up from your book and gaze at the other end of the room for a moment. If you do this you should never be troubled with eye fatigue. Many people who read eight or more hours a day do not experience eye fatigue because they consistently practice good reading hygiene.

There is also the matter of where not to read. Reading on any kind of moving vehicle is not a good idea. The vibrations produced by a train or bus, for example, might cause severe strain and can do irreparable damage to your eyes. In such a situation you can't possibly do a good job of reading and will probably begin to establish poor reading habits. Give up reading on trains and buses, for it is scarcely a pleasant experience and may prove a time waster or health hazard in the long run. Reading in bed is also a poor practice. It is difficult to find a good light for reading in bed, and most people cannot easily manage a comfortable reading position for very long. In addition, reading in bed tends to make you sleepy, and a sleepy reader is not an efficient reader. It is foolish to read yourself to sleep because good reading requires a mind that is able to concentrate. Even if you don't intend to do "good" reading in bed and feel that "reading for pleasure" doesn't require much concentration, you still aren't helping your reading habits; when you read in bed you are breaking the training rules for efficient reading. If you are going to read, choose a fairly upright armchair or a comfortable desk chair. Then sit up and pay attention. You will find that you are much more able to concentrate and actually do a better job than if you are in a slumped or reclining position. You will also be more comfortable.

The size of print and the color and quality of the paper are other important factors in reading. Most good books nowadays are a joy to read because they are printed on dull white paper and in clear, readable type. Some cheap books, however, and many old books are printed in too small type on paper that is too gray or yellow or shiny. If you must read them, be sure to rest your eyes frequently while doing so. Follow the same procedure when reading on a microfilm machine.

One last word about the hygiene of reading. In general, the health of your eyes ordinarily depends on the overall health of your body. Good food and plenty of sleep and relaxation are tremendously important, as is an alert mind, free from tension and distractions. You cannot expect to move quickly and efficiently through the pages of a book if you are physically under par. The good reader is a healthy reader.

Record your rate here: _____

Average rate for Chapter 3: 310 wpm. Turn to the Comprehension Check on page 112.

Application Exercise: Chapter 3

Changing Rates

You have now read three chapters and have a fair idea of what you can do with relatively easy reading. Below is a selection such as you might find in an old psychology textbook. Although it is old, it is relevant to understanding many twentieth-century writers who use the stream-of-consciousness technique. The idea for the technique started with William James.

The selections will require slow and careful reading, a shift to a reading gear different from the one you have been using on this book. You may have to refer to a dictionary, underline certain words, jot down a few notes, and reread a passage or two. Try to master the material, time yourself to get some idea of how much of a change in reading speed you have had to make, and answer the questions at the end of the selection.

Words appearing in the vocabulary check on p. 20 are underlined.

William James's Comments on the Stream of Consciousness

The order of our study must be analytic. We are now prepared to begin the introspective study of the adult consciousness itself.

The Fundamental Fact. The first and foremost concrete fact which every one will affirm to belong to his inner experience is the fact that *consciousness of some sort goes on. 'States of mind' succeed each other in him.* If we could say in English "it thinks," as we say "it rains" or "it blows," we should be stating the fact most simply and with the minimum of assumption. As we cannot, we must simply say that *thought goes on.*

Four Characters in Consciousness. How does it go on? We notice immediately four important characters in the process, of which it shall be the duty of the present chapter to treat in a general way:

(1) Every "state" tends to be part of a personal consciousness.

(2) Within each personal consciousness states are always changing.

(3) Each personal consciousness is sensibly continuous.

(4) It is interested in some parts of its object to the exclusion of others, and welcomes or rejects—*chooses* from among them, in a word—all the while.

In considering these four points successively, we shall have to plunge *in medias res* as regards our nomenclature and use psychological terms which can only be adequately defined in later chapters of the book.

(1) When I say *every "state" or "thought" is part of a personal consciousness,* "personal consciousness" is one of the terms in question. Its meaning we know so long as no one asks us to define it, but to give an accurate account of it is the most difficult of philosophic tasks. This task we must confront in the next chapter; here a preliminary word will suffice.

In this room—this lecture-room, say—there are a multitude of thoughts, yours and mine, some of which cohere mutually, and some not. They are as little each-for-itself and reciprocally independent as they are all-belonging-together. They are neither: no one of them is separate, but each belongs with certain others and with none beside. My thought belongs with *my* other thoughts, and your thought with *your* other thoughts.

(2) *Consciousness is in constant change.* I do not mean by this to say that no one state of mind has any duration—even if true, that would be hard to establish. What I wish to lay stress on is this, that *no state once gone can recur and be identical with what it was before. A permanently existing "Idea" which makes its appearance before the footlights of consciousness at periodical intervals is as mythological an entity as the Jack of Spades.*

(3) *Within each personal consciousness, thought is sensibly continuous.* I can only define "continuous" as that which is without breach, crack, or division.

Consciousness, then, does not appear to itself chopped up in bits. Such words as "chain" or "train" do not describe it fitly as it presents itself in the first instance. It is nothing jointed; it flows. A "river" or a "stream" are the metaphors by which it is most naturally described. *In talking of it hereafter, let us call it the stream of thought, of consciousness, or of subjective life.*

(500 words)*   Rate _____.

After you have mastered the preceding paragraphs from the chapter on "The Stream of Consciousness" from William James's *The Principles of Psychology* (1890), take the test below to check your comprehension.

Directions: mark with a J those characteristics of consciousness James mentioned; mark with an N those characteristics James either did not mention or would not agree with.

_____ 1. Every "state" tends to be a part of personal consciousness.
_____ 2. Consciousness proceeds by constant and recurring effort, a conscious and deliberate effort of the will.
_____ 3. Within each personal consciousness, states are always changing.
_____ 4. No matter how one perceives it, the sensation of green is always green, cologne is always cologne.
_____ 5. Consciousness of self is a permanently existing idea.
_____ 6. Each personal consciousness is sensibly continuous.
_____ 7. Each consciousness is interested in parts of its object to the exclusion of others.
_____ 8. The words "chain" or "train" are as appropriate as "stream" to describe consciousness as it presents itself.
_____ 9. Changes in quality of the consciousness are often abrupt but explainable.
_____ 10. We have the means of ascertaining three kinds of thought: yours, mine, and thought-in-itself.

James's characteristics are first, third, sixth, seventh.

*Use one half the rate given in the table, letting a time of one minute equal 500 words per minute, not 1000 words per minute.

Application Exercise: Chapter 4

Reading Logically

While no one can tell you what word groupings are natural for you, you can convince yourself there are groupings by trying a test. Count by twos the words in the first paragraph of Chapter 4. The test shows that natural groups don't come in pairs.

Underlined words appear in the vocabulary check on page 20.
Read the following paragraph three times, thinking in terms of logical groupings. Record the number of seconds for each trial.

Poe on the Story's Single Effect (1842)

A skillful literary artist has constructed a tale. If wise, he has not fashioned his thoughts to accommodate his incidents; but having conceived with deliberate care, a certain unique or single *effect* to be <u>wrought out</u> he then invents such incidents—he then combines such events as may best aid him in establishing this <u>preconceived</u> effect. If his very initial sentence tend not to the outbringing of this effect, then he has failed in his first step. In the whole composition, there should be no word written of which the tendency, direct or indirect, is not to the one <u>pre-established</u> design.

First trial: _____ seconds
Second trial: _____ seconds
Third trial: _____ seconds

Now read the paragraph a fourth time and underline the groupings
Practice this kind of exercise frequently by rereading articles that you find interesting in the daily paper.
Continue your practice on the following paragraphs:

Howells on Realism (1891)

Let fiction cease to lie about life; let it portray men and women as they are, <u>actuated</u> by the motives and the passions in the measure we all know; let it leave off painting dolls and working them by springs and wires; let it show the different interests in their true proportions; let it forbear to preach pride and <u>revenge</u>, <u>folly</u> and insanity, egotism and prejudice, but frankly own these for what they are, in whatever figures and occasions they appear; let it not put on fine literary airs; let it speak the dialect, the language, that most Americans know—the language of <u>unaffected</u> people everywhere—and there can be no doubt of an unlimited future, not only of delightfulness but of usefulness, for it.

First trial: _____ seconds
Second trial: _____ seconds
Third trial: _____ seconds

Now read the paragraph a fourth time and underline the groupings.

Henry James on Fiction (1884)

The only reason for the existence of a novel is that it does attempt to represent life. When it <u>relinquishes</u> this attempt, the same attempt that we see on the canvas of the painter, it will have arrived at a very strange pass. It is not expected of the picture that it will make itself humble in order to be forgiven; and the <u>analogy</u> between the art of the painter and the art of the novelist is, so far as I am able to see, complete. Their inspiration is the same, their process (allowing for the different quality of the vehicle), is the same, their success is the same. They may learn from each other, they may explain and sustain each other. Their cause is the same, and the honour of one is the honour of another.

First trial: _____ seconds
Second trial: _____ seconds
Third trial: _____ seconds

Now read the paragraph a fourth time and underline the groupings.

Vocabulary in Context I

The words below have been selected from the Application Exercises in Chapters 1, 3, and 4. Match the words with their definitions. Write the number of each word next to its definition. The Answer Key is on page 134.

Words from Chapter 1

1. linear sequence
2. practitioner
3. accessible
4. provoked
5. goaded
6. latterly
7. puny
8. ailment

_____ aroused
_____ lately
_____ an arrangement in one dimension
_____ mild illness
_____ easily approached
_____ urged
_____ professional artist or writer
_____ very small

Words from Chapter 3

1. consciousness
2. assumption
3. *in medias res*
4. nomenclature
5. cohere
6. mutually
7. reciprocally
8. mythological
9. entity
10. breach
11. subjective

_____ jointly
_____ names of things
_____ of one's own mind
_____ based on ancient story
_____ opening
_____ stick together
_____ anything that exists
_____ in exchange
_____ awareness
_____ in the middle of things
_____ supposition

Words from Chapter 4

1. wrought out
2. preconceived
3. pre-established
4. actuated
5. revenge
6. folly
7. unaffected
8. relinquishes
9. analogy

_____ decided upon beforehand
_____ punish in return
_____ gives up
_____ not changed
_____ foolishness
_____ formed beforehand
_____ point-by-point relationship
_____ put into action
_____ made or shaped

5 *Shifting Gears*

If you are making an emergency trip to the doctor, you do not proceed at the same leisurely rate that you might use for a holiday drive in the country. You move as rapidly as you can because getting to the doctor is your main objective. During a drive in the country you take your time. You may stop now and then to examine more closely some object that has engaged your attention. Your progress is casual; you relax and enjoy yourself. On your trip to the doctor, however, nothing distracts your attention. All your faculties are concentrated on the business at hand, which is to get to a certain destination as quickly as you can.

So it is with reading: There are different speeds for different purposes. Although this may seem too obvious to mention, a great many people, including some who should know better, seem to ignore it. Either they plod through an Agatha Christie story at the same speed they would employ for an article on relativity in some scientific journal or, less frequently, they are discouraged because they can't race through difficult material at the same rate they use for light fiction.

When you change from one kind of reading matter to another, you can and should change your speed of reading. In fact, in order to read widely in many fields you have to read at different rates of speed. You go along in low gear until you master the difficult and unfamiliar books in a field, and then you shift to high gear as you begin to get the subject under control. For difficult passages you will sometimes have to slip into second gear, and when you run into a popularized version of your topic, you can coast along. Not all reading offers the same degree of difficulty or requires the same reading speed.

Do not ask, "How fast should I read?" on the assumption that everyone can read at some certain rate. Reading rate is strictly individual. There are no set standards; there is no ideal speed; there is no correct speed; there is no one right way. Speed varies according to the difficulty of the material and the purpose of the individual reader.

Although they sometimes overlap, there are three distinct purposes that one may have for reading. A textbook in sociology dispenses information; a novel like *Moby-Dick* provides enrichment of life; and a detective story offers relaxation. To some degree, each purpose requires a different method of reading.

If you begin to read a technical work on a subject with which you are not very familiar, you must read slowly and master the details, for here you are reading to obtain information; you are reading for data that you intend to put to good use. You have to take time to master the special vocabulary of the subject, and you have to read painstakingly to understand the relation of one aspect of the subject to another. The chances are that you will also have to proceed rather slowly because you will need to take notes.

When you read something like biography or history you also have to go slowly, because again you are reading for information. Suppose you read Edith Hamilton's book *The Greek Way*. You would start slowly and proceed carefully, keeping in mind the important facts about history and philosophy. But you would be able to increase your speed gradually as you read more and more. You would find that you had developed a familiarity with Hamilton's operational system. Each new book about Greek history or philosophy you later read would help you fill in some of the missing details, but there would be some repetition that would permit more rapid reading.

You also read for information when you use a reference book, but in such a book you don't read through the whole thing to find out what you want. For example, it would be absurd to read through an entire book on Greek history to find information on Socrates. The best method, if there were no index, would be to skim through the book until you came to the material relating to your subject. Then, reading for information, you would probably read slowly and carefully.

Speaking quite generally, the things one reads for enrichment of life are works of literature—poems, novels, short stories, plays, and essays. At least the best books of this sort are serious works of art. If you want to get from them the most they have to give, you should read with all the concentration and awareness at your command. Each detail, each shade of meaning, each character, each paragraph was fashioned with special care; if you rush along, you will inevitably miss much of what the author was careful to put there for you to see. Authors are often trying to share an important truth they have discovered, often in the process of writing. You read to find it.

When you are reading an ordinary adventure or detective story, you are reading for relaxation. The story may or may not give you new and valuable insight into life, but it usually is interesting enough to keep your attention. You read for the story—who gets the girl, what happens to Sam Spade, when will Tom deliver the winning goal for the team? Therefore, even though you are reading for relaxation, you should read rapidly. This type of literature does not call for slow and careful reading.

Remember, you can consciously change your reading rate and should set about destroying any mental barriers that keep you in low gear all the time. Only when you are able to shift easily will you be able to give the various materials you read the varying amounts of time and attention that they deserve. And only then will you be able to understand Sir Francis Bacon's famous saying: "Some books are to be tasted, others to be swallowed, and some few to be chewed and digested."

Average rate for Chapter 5: 325 wpm. Turn to the Comprehension Check on page 114.

Application Exercise: Chapter 5

Savoring the Style

Here is another selection you will need <u>to read slowly and carefully</u>. Though it was written by Francis Bacon in 1597 and contains a few words that may send you to the dictionary, it provides an excellent example of a terse and concise sentence structure and the force, elegance, and clarity of great English prose. Savor the style as you read it—and time yourself to get an accurate idea of how you are able to shift gears according to the difficulty of the material and the purpose for which you read. (Vocabulary words are underlined.)

Of Studies

Studies serve for delight, for ornament, and for ability. Their chief use for delight is in privateness and retiring; for ornament, is in discourse; and for ability, is in the judgment and <u>disposition</u> of business; for expert men can execute, and perhaps judge of particulars, one by one; but the general counsels, and the plots and <u>marshaling</u> affairs come best from those that are learned. To spend too much time in studies is <u>sloth</u>; to use them too much for ornament is <u>affection</u>; to make judgment wholly by their rules is the <u>humor</u> of a scholar. They perfect nature, and are perfected by experience; for natural abilities are like natural plants, that need <u>pruning</u> by study; and studies themselves do give forth directions too much at large, except they be bounded in by experience. Crafty men condemn studies, simple men admire them, and wise men use them; for they teach not their own use; but that is a wisdom without them and above them, won by observation. Read not to contradict and <u>confute</u> nor to believe and take for granted, nor to find talk and discourse, but to weigh and consider. Some books are to be tasted, others to be swallowed, and some few to be chewed and digested; that is, some books are to be read only in parts; others to be read but not curiously (carefully), and some few to be read wholly, and with diligence and attention. Some books also may be read by deputy, and extracts made of them by others; but that would be only in the less important arguments and the meaner sort of books; else distilled books are, like common distilled waters, flashy things. Reading maketh a full man; conference a ready man; and writing an exact man. And, therefore, if a man write little, he had need have a great memory; if he confer little, he had need have a present <u>wit</u>; and if he read little, he had need have much cunning, to seem to know that he doth not. Histories make men wise; poets, witty; the mathematics, subtle; natural philosophy, deep; moral, grave; logic and rhetoric, able to contend; *Abeunt studia in mores* (studies form manners). Nay, there is no stand or <u>impediment</u> in the wit but may be <u>wrought out</u> by fit studies; like as diseases of the body may have appropriate exercises. Bowling is good for the stone and reins, shooting for the lungs and breast, gentle walking for the stomach, riding for the head and the like. So if a man's wit be wandering, let him study the mathematics; for in demonstrations, if his wit be called away never so little, he must begin again. If his wit be not apt to distinguish or find differences, let him study the schoolmen; for they are *cymini sectores* (hairsplitters). If he be not apt to beat over matters, and to call up one thing to prove and illustrate another, let him study the lawyers' cases; so every defect of the mind may have a special receipt.

Sir Francis Bacon
Record your rate here _____ *(500 words in this selection)**

Use notebook paper to answer the following:

1. If your rate is slower here than on other material, explain why.

2. A serious reader would read *Of Studies* for information, for enrichment of life, for relaxation, or for a combination of these purposes. Can you explain each purpose.

3. Prepare answers to the following comprehension questions:
    a. What do you think Bacon meant by saying that the chief use of studying for delight is "in privateness and retiring"?
    b. What does he mean by saying that the use of studying for ornament is "in discourse"?
    c. What does he mean by saying that studies serve ability?
    d. There is no conclusion to Bacon's essay. What would his summary contain?
    e. In what sense could one spend too much time in studies?
    f. What does he mean by the statement that "studies themselves do give forth direction too much at large, except they be bounded by experience"?
    g. Cite examples from your own reading of books to be chewed, tasted, and swallowed.

*Use one half the rate given in the table, letting a time of one minute equal 500 words per minute, not 1000 words per minute.

6 *Skimming Along*

The phrase "skimming along" is an appealing one, suggesting an effortless swiftness and an easy smoothness of motion. "Skimming through a book" also has a pleasant sound, and many people think that there must be an easy method of doing this kind of reading, some method that would automatically solve their reading problems. They mistake the nature of this pleasant-sounding process.

There are no mechanical rules for skimming that will enable you to do it in some easy, automatic way. There is no special way of flipping the pages or flexing your eyes; you cannot skim by reading the second word of every third paragraph; you cannot skim by reading every tenth page or by reading every fourth chapter. There simply are no such mechanical rules for skimming, none at all.

There *are* rules for skimming, however, though they are not mechanical ones. By far the most important is this: *Skim for a definite purpose.* If you know what you are looking for, if you have a question in mind and read to find the answer, if you search for specific information, you will be able to skim successfully. You know exactly what you are looking for and omit what does not suit your purpose. That is the one and only reason you can skim a book faster than you can read it through.

Much of the skimming you will want to do will be in books of nonfiction. In such books you should start with the table of contents. Examine it carefully to find the chapters or sections you think will best suit your immediate purpose. Decide what you will omit entirely, what you will glance through, and what you will read thoroughly. Next, turn to the particular chapters that interest you and examine the "signposts," the chapter headings and subheadings, to note if possible where the information is you are looking for. When you begin to read a particular section, let your eyes run rapidly down the page to seek the information you desire. When you come to a passage that appears promising, settle down and read as carefully as is necessary in order to get the full meaning. The author, a few years ago was writing a long paper on the nineteenth-century vogue of mesmerism (now known as *hypnotism*). Having to read hundreds of books and articles, he became so sensitive to the word *mesmerism* that it literally seemed to jump at him every time he skimmed a page. When he found his "signpost," mesmerism, he would backtrack and carefully read the two or three sentences before and after it to see how the word had been used in context. Skimming, thus, is not different from ordinary reading. It's just that while skimming you omit the irrelevant portions.

Suppose you wanted to find out how many Presbyterians there are in the United States. Would you flip through the pages of the *World Almanac* until you found that information? If you did you would be wasting time. The first thing you would do would be to turn to the index and look up "Presbyterians." Then you would turn to the appropriate page, run your eye down the proper column, and quickly find the figure you were looking for. You would be doing a simple kind of skimming.

When you skim any book of nonfiction you do essentially the same thing just described for the *World Almanac*. You first turn your attention to the index or table of contents. Experienced book skimmers will tell you that there is nothing more helpful to them in skimming than the index of a book.

The daily newspaper lends itself very readily to skimming. Although many newspapers print most of the news that is fit to print, not all of it is worth reading every day. Unfortunately, some newspapers do not have an adequate index, which means you must turn each page laboriously and glance at each headline to see what is worth reading. Such headline reading is skimming in one of its most common forms. After you have read a newspaper each day for a week or so, and are familiar with its various sections, you learn to turn immediately to those parts of the paper that interest you most. You know that the business section is always in the same approximate location and that the sports columns and the "funnies" and the editorials all have their particular spot. In a short time you can learn to skim the paper with ease, because you know just what you are looking for and you know where to find it.

The ability to skim a newspaper, which you have probably already developed, should be applied to skimming magazines and books as well. Magazines are easy to skim because they usually have a table of contents that enables you to decide quite easily what to read and what to skip. If you read the subtitles of the articles in a magazine, you can get a pretty good idea of their purpose and content. Take, for example, a magazine article entitled, "Give It Back to the Indians." The title is intriguing but undescriptive; it doesn't tell you what the article is about. Should you or should you not read it? Look at the subtitle: "High taxes, hot summers, and a maddening pace make Manhattan Island a perfect climate for neuroses." Here is practically a summary of the article. It reveals the purpose of the writer and even offers a clue to the humorous style of writing.

Skimming through printed matter is not as easy as skimming a flat rock over water. There is more to it than a mechanical flick of the wrist. Nor is skimming like taking the cream off a bottle of milk. It is more like scanning the shelves of a supermarket to find what you came to buy. You know why you're there, you know what you're looking for, and you look for that alone. This is skimming.

Record your rate here: _____

Average rate for Chapter 6: 350 wpm. Turn to the Comprehension Check on page 115.

Application Exercise: Chapter 6

Searching Accurately

Exercises in skimming are bound to be artificial since only individual readers can know the particular purpose they are skimming for. On the other hand, some skimming exercises can be beneficial if they give readers practice in moving their eyes rapidly down the page and teach them how to search accurately. During part of the time you spend on this practice, try to catch the feeling of your eyes selecting significant phrases. Think of your eyes moving as you read the first two selections. It is not a good idea to get into the habit of thinking about eye movements, so try it only once or twice. *Skim as rapidly as possible.* (Words appearing in the vocabulary check are underscored.)

Mark Twain in Cincinnati. About how long did he live there?

Although his arrival date is not certain, Mark Twain probably got off the train in Cincinnati on October 24, 1856, just five weeks before his twenty-first birthday. He worked for a printer all that fall and winter, and on April 15, 1857, he boarded the *Paul Jones* bound for New Orleans.

Sherwood Anderson in Springfield. When did he live there?

When Sherwood Anderson came to study at the Wittenberg Academy he lived with his brother in a huge boarding house with a large cast of characters. Although he was not to write about them for at least fifteen years, the characters he met on September 11, 1899, on 153 South Factory Street, in Springfield, Ohio, meant a good deal to him.

William Dean Howells in a Log Cabin. When did he live there?

Although William Dean Howells wrote *My Year in a Log Cabin* in 1888, the site of the cabin itself was not known to today's historians until 1976, when a land deed made out to Howell's uncles turned up in the Greene County Courthouse. The deed was dated 1849; it was the next year that the Howells family lived on the banks of the Little Miami River near the Upper Bellbrook Road.

The Junto Club: How many years after it was founded did the Junto Club form a subscription library?

The Junto Club, a social and debating society, founded by Benjamin Franklin at Philadelphia (1727), was first known as the Leather Aprons. The workingmen who were members kept it going as a vital force in Philadelphia's cultural affairs for forty years. A subscription library was formed by the club in 1731, the first American public library.

Insulin: Why is insulin an aid in curing diabetes?

Insulin is a hormone <u>extract</u> obtained from the islets of Langerhans of the pancreas of animals (chiefly pigs and oxen), used in treating diabetes and in regulating the <u>metabolism</u> of glucose in the blood and urine.

Color: What is the most striking feature of color?

Color is the evaluation by the visual sense of that quality of an object or substance with respect to light (reflected or transmitted), expressed in terms of hue, chroma, and brightness. Generally the most striking feature is the hue, which gives the color its name, qualified as pale, dark, dull, light, and so on.

Simulacrum: How is it different from an exact replica?

A simulacrum is an image, something that has a similar form; a shadowy likeness of something without its substance. Carlyle said that it was time for man to "quit *simulacrae* and return to fact."

Monaco: When did the rule of the Rainier family begin?

Monaco is the smallest country in Europe, having an area of eight square miles, bounded by the French Alps and the Mediterranean. Its casino is the gambling center of Europe. The family of Prince Rainier of Monaco has ruled since 1327, and the Prince is one of the few <u>titular</u> sovereigns left in Europe.

Woodrow Wilson: How long was he president of Princeton?

Woodrow Wilson, the twenty-eighth President, was born in 1856 in Staunton, Virginia. After receiving degrees from Princeton in New Jersey, the University of Virginia in Charlottesville, and Johns Hopkins in Baltimore, he taught history and government at Bryn Mawr near Philadelphia, at Wesleyan in Middletown, Connecticut, and, lastly, at his <u>alma mater</u> Princeton, where he served as president from 1902 to 1910.

World War I Peace Treaty: Was Germany to be allowed an army and navy?

By terms of the peace treaty, Germany agreed to restore Alsace-Lorraine to France, recognized the independence of Poland, the free city of Danzig, Czechoslovakia, and Austria. Germany also surrendered all her colonies to the Allied powers. Compulsory military service was prohibited, and the size of her army and navy was fixed. Finally, Germany was obliged to make such <u>restitution</u> and <u>reparation</u> for war damage as might be determined.

7 Concentrating

To read efficiently you have to concentrate on what you are reading. You cannot read well if your mind wanders off to other things. If you are involved in a serious emotional problem or going through a nerve-shattering period of indecision, it is quite possible that you won't be an efficient reader. The reason is one we've all heard a thousand times: "I can't keep my mind on my work." Most people, however, are not so tormented by personal problems that they cannot read well if they set their minds to it. Unless your situation is distracting in some unusual way, you can learn to concentrate on your reading as well as the best.

You have already learned that when you read efficiently you read intensively. The act of reading occupies skillful readers completely. They simply do not allow themselves to be distracted by outside influences. Even if you don't consider yourself such a reader now, it is probable that if you plan to study you arrange a suitable place where you will not be bothered or interrupted too frequently. Even if you are reading simply for pleasure you generally attempt to keep distracting influences to a minimum. In short, you know that good concentration depends on your ability to control and direct your attention.

If you try to listen to the radio at the same time you study a history lesson, you are going to find it difficult to give full and satisfactory attention to your reading. Although some investigators have shown that workers on an assembly line can sometimes increase their output if they listen to music while they work, other investigators have shown that the real reason workers produce more is because they know they are in an experiment and the experiment gives them incentive. It is true that you *can* read and listen to music, but you make it more difficult to concentrate by doing so. Even if people could condition themselves to reading in an artillery barrage, they ought not to choose willingly that atmosphere. Certainly inefficient readers fight against themselves when they try to read and listen to a quiz program. As they cannot give full attention to either activity, neither do they derive full enjoyment from either. Readers whose attention is divided cannot read at their efficient best.

As you have already noted, you can probably concentrate well enough if you seek an environment that gives you half a chance. Of course, not all background noise can be eliminated when you read. There is bound to be some. Both Thomas Carlyle and Marcel Proust tried unsuccessfully to insulate themselves from the noise and confusion of the outside world by writing in cork-lined chambers. It is enough to try to eliminate as many really distracting influences as possible. If you can learn to lose yourself in the printed page you won't be bothered by minor distractions. Watch twelve-year-old children read comic books if you want to see an example of intensive reading. No minor distractions trouble them! Try to get their attention. They will not hear you until they are finished. They are quite literally "out of this world." You could drop a bomb, and they would emerge from the debris with the paper still before them—reading intensively. Their taste in reading matter may not be the best, but their ability to concentrate is worth trying to imitate.

Some people find that they cannot pay attention and have a tendency to daydream when they read relatively uninteresting matter. They often find that they have gone through three or four pages without remembering a word. One cure for this is to stop reading and deliberately seek some distraction, then return to the book with renewed attention. Get up and walk around, raid the icebox, play the piano, count your pocket change—anything. Then pick up the book and take up from where you left off. No one can tell you exactly what to do if your mind wanders when you read, because to some degree this problem is an individual one you must work out for yourself. The important thing is to do something about it, not just tell yourself, as so many people do: "I can't concentrate."

Perhaps the best general advice is: Don't mix play and work. Apply yourself to your task and keep going as long as you can give the job full attention. You should be able to read for at least an hour or two without interruption. When you begin to feel that you are not getting as much out of your reading as you ought to, let up for a while. But if there is more work remaining to be done, make the rest period short. It is surprising how quickly you can refresh your mind by turning to some thing entirely different for a few minutes. It doesn't take long to get your mind out of a rut, and when you return to the book, you will be alert and ready to go at it with a mind refreshed.

If this suggestion does not solve your problem, there is another thing you can do. Form the habit of reading in the same place each time you read. Make this place, whether it be a table at the public library or a desk in your study, a place for "concentrated" reading. Write your letters and complete your crossword puzzles somewhere else. After you have tried this practice for a week or two, you will find that your habits will begin to work for you—which doesn't mean, of course, that they will take over the whole process. There is still the matter of will power.

One of the principal things to remember about concentration is that you yourself must be willing to exercise the self-discipline necessary to control your reading habits. While it is true that a favorable environment is a great help, the main thing is this: Condition yourself to reading intensively.

Record your rate here: _____
Average rate for Chapter 7: 360 wpm. Turn to the Comprehension
Check on page 116.

Application Exercise: Chapter 7

Performing Automatically

It is difficult to examine an action objectively if it has become something you perform automatically and without thinking. Concentration is such an act. When you are highly motivated, when you have a keen desire to accomplish a task, you direct all your powers to succeeding, and you may lose track of the conditions of sound, smell, touch, taste, and sometimes even sight during the act.

Here are a few simple tricks that require a high degree of concentration—and a relatively small amount of mental exertion. Try them to see if you can determine what conditions help you to concentrate best.

1. Hold a watch to your ear and slowly move it away until you can no longer hear it. Then hold it at the maximum hearing distance and listen to the consecutive ticks for thirty seconds. At the end of that time you will probably realize that you can now move the watch even further away and still hear the ticks. Can you account for this?
2. Using a rubber band, fasten a paper napkin over a drinking glass. Put a penny on the napkin and in two minutes see how many different holes you can burn in the napkin without letting the penny drop into the glass.
3. Simultaneously move your right hand in a circle over your stomach and pat your head with your left hand. When you succeed, change hands and reverse the process; then reverse the process every ten pats. Why does this trick become easier as you practice it?
4. Look at the second hand of a watch and count the number of your heartbeats per minute.
5. Lie on your back and hold a book at arm's length above you. How long can you concentrate on the reading before your muscles tire?
6. Read the following number once and then look away and repeat it: 55059642. Try the same with these numbers: 47247307, 05459417, 51319176, 51468938.
7. Read the following lists rapidly and pick out the one item that is different:
   robin, sparrow, bear, oriole, wren, lark (read more rapidly!)
   oak, elm, maple, birch, hickory, ruler (keep moving!)
   rabbit, possum, horse, mouse, eagle, squirrel
   Reagan, Eisenhower, Carter, Mailer, Johnson, Roosevelt
   Dickens, Thackery, Longfellow, Emerson, Edison, Thoreau
8. Once before it was suggested you count words by twos. Now count the words in the first paragraph of Chapter 7 by twos. You will find that the natural word groups don't fall in pairs, and it will take considerable concentration to do the job.
9. Answer the following questions about overcoming boredom: (interest = concentration)
   a. Are you just reading a set number of pages or are you trying to understand the material?
   b. Challenge yourself. Can you turn the author's concepts into opposites and ask yourself why the opposites aren't true?

31

c. Some material needs to be mastered. Do you habitually pick out the one or two things a day that need mastering?

d. When you read, ". . . from the above it follows logically," do you anticipate the author's message and compare your version with the original?

e. Do you ever begin by finding very elementary books about a subject? Such books can help you master basic concepts and give you a firm foundation.

f. Have you tried reading around a subject? If you read how James Watson helped discover the biological code in *The Double Helix*, it may revive a flagging interest in biology. A trip to the zoo or the botanical garden may do the same.

8 *Using Signposts*

The ability to comprehend means the ability to translate printed symbols into meaningful ideas. Readers comprehend a book in terms of the ideas—gained through actual life situations and through reading—that have meaning for them. The idea of relativity, for example, has little meaning for most readers. Ideas of love or hate, however, have very definite meaning for everyone, because everyone has experienced these things. Readers understand most fully when they have a rich background of experience in the subject they are reading.

It would be foolish to try to improve comprehension by enriching your background of experience in the few pages of this chapter, but it is possible to offer some suggestions for understanding better what you read.

Suppose you wish to digest a book as thoroughly as possible. Your first task will be to direct your attention to finding the central thought of each chapter, section, and paragraph by making use of all the author's "signposts." Several kinds of these signposts should be obvious to every reader. For example, the signpost that marks the central thought of this chapter is the title, "Using Signposts." Divisions within chapters may be clearly defined by subheadings, usually set off in a special type. A biology book, for example, may have a chapter entitled "Charles Darwin," with such subheadings for the chapter as "Darwin's Life," "Darwin's Work," and "Darwin's Influence." The last subheading may be further divided into "Contemporary Influence" and "Historical Influence." Another kind of signpost, not so easily noted, is the paragraph topic sentence, which is quite often the first sentence in a paragraph. If it is the first sentence, the purpose it serves will commonly be twofold: to indicate exactly how the author's thought is being carried forward from the previous paragraph and to introduce the idea of what is to follow. In other words, it concludes one unit of the author's thought and begins another. As such, it holds a key position in the pattern of sentences on the page. It is, therefore, a signpost for which we should look. Determining the author's topic ideas is crucial to good reading comprehension.

Another suggestion that can lead to more complete understanding of what you read is this: Sift ideas. That is, try to determine what is significant and what is not in the material. A good reader working for thorough understanding makes a constant attempt to find the author's main ideas and to relate the minor ideas to it. In order to decide what is worth remembering, a reader separates the frills—the unimportant facts and details, which are offered only as extra evidence to reinforce a point already made—from the main ideas. Someone has said that the sign of a truly successful executive is an empty wastebasket at the start of a day, and a full one at the end. Similarly, successful readers discard the unimportant things they read.

Suppose an author begins a paragraph like this: "Youth, as a rule, has an immense reserve of strength and thus has the ability to cope with changed conditions." This, of course, is a generalization, and it will need facts and illustrations to back it up. Suppose that, later in the paragraph, the author wrote, "On treacherous White Lake, three teen-age campers were able to cling to their capsized boat for twelve hours." This is an illustration offered as evidence of the truth of the earlier statement about youth. When the two statements are separated and discussed, as they are here, it is easy to see the relationship between them. A good reader constantly finds such relationships between main ideas and details. Poor readers, on the other hand, rarely bother to do so. As a result of this failure to train themselves, they not only misinterpret the author's meaning and thereby reveal themselves as poor readers, but they also carry into their everyday lives a mass of misconceptions and wrong ideas.

People who form their opinions mostly on the basis of what they read in newspaper headlines are examples of readers who often fail to make logical connections between facts and generalizations. Headlines are "eyecatchers"—that is, in a limited number of words and in an appealing or even sensational manner, they must tell the reader what is newsworthy. Thus, they sometimes distort the news by making generalizations that the facts may not support. For instance, when a doctor told a public health group the results of an attempt to help autistic children, the headline and the first three paragraphs of the news story that treated the doctor's speech read as follows:

Autistic Children Can Relate

Chapel Hill, N.C.—Seated beside the therapist, five-year-old Mary squirms, lolls, bobs her head, and focuses on thin air. She is autistic, unable to relate to people or things.

Then the therapist calls her name until Mary looks at her. Touching her lips, the doctor pleads with Mary to touch her own lips and say the word "lips." Mary finally obeys.

Mary's parents observe unseen in another room. They too are part of her therapy.

Readers who stop there form their opinions on ideas unsupported by facts. The parts of the article they have read may lead them to think that there may be a sure treatment for autistic children. Yet the article goes on to say that because of the severity of the problem most of the children will never "make it" in the normal sense. The headlines and beginning paragraphs lead the reader to one opinion; the facts, which follow, lead to another. To comprehend the whole article the reader needs to examine the relationship between facts and generalizations.

Good comprehension demands that you think of reading as a constant searching out of meaning and that you sift and evaluate and select among the facts and ideas on a page—noting what is most relevant, and discarding the unneeded. Is anything more important to you on the road to successful reading?

Record your rate here: _____
Average rate for Chapter 8: 370 wpm. Turn to the Comprehension
Check on page 117.

Application Exercise: Chapter 8

Getting to the Nub

Read rapidly and find the main topic of each of the following paragraphs. The main topic may or may not be a single sentence. More likely it will be a modified summary of the paragraph. An illustration follows:

When Ernest Hemingway used Sherwood Anderson's letter of introduction to Gertrude Stein, they became if not good friends at least close acquaintants, and even when Gertrude told Ernest to begin writing all over again and concentrate, they were still close. When she was a godparent at the baptism of his son, one would have imagined that they would stay friends for life—but it was not to be. Before the flowers of friendship faded, friendship faded.

Main idea: At first Hemingway and Stein were friends but their friendship faded.

1. Katherine Anne Porter's stories show her heroine's vulnerability to an evil world. They were insightful attempts to show that endurance triumphs. They revealed, in cyclical descriptions of a woman's whole life, the clash between a woman and the society she lives in. They also reveal the conflict between a woman and the forlorn quality of her hopes.

Main idea:

2. Eudora Welty does not have easy answers to the problems the characters in her short stories face, but she approaches her subject with compassion and humor. Her characters are not better or happier for being recognized or for falling in love, but in the manner of an impressionistic painter she makes experience available.

Main idea:

3. Flannery O'Connor's stories seem to focus on comic perversion. In "Good Country People" both the lonely educated woman with an artificial leg and the smooth-talking Bible salesman pervert their true selves, and in the seduction scene there is a perversion of love that would be, if it weren't for the comic elements, squalid and tragic.

36

Main idea:

4. One hears that a Helen Santmyer novel is all about descriptions of wallpaper and rope manufacture in Xenia, Ohio. But it is a great deal more than that. The point of the descriptions is to record in such telling detail the life of the nineteenth century that it will capture the spirit of the time in as realistic a manner as possible. She succeeds in riveting our attention to the details that make life what it is.

Main idea:

5. Willa Cather's biographer, James Woodress, says, "I know of no other writer of this century who is more likely to go on being read than Willa Cather." She published nineteen volumes in her lifetime and there have been at least a dozen biographies of this extraordinarily energetic woman from the provinces. She is best known for evoking the pioneer spirit of her childhood in Nebraska, revealing that spirit in her <u>epic</u> romances and excursions into the past.

Main idea:

9 *Computing Your Motivation*

Programs in reading for speed have always been inclined to use whatever motivational devices work. In fact, it was in experiments with mechanical devices in pioneer reading programs at such universities as Iowa, Harvard, and Chicago in the years following World War II that speed-reading programs began. Then certain devices that had proved useful in training military personnel were converted for civilian use. There was a machine called a *tachistoscope* (*tachis* = speed; *scope* = viewer) that flashed words or objects (such as *friendly* and *enemy aircraft*) on a screen at speeds up to one hundredth of a second, or a machine that sent a shutter down a page of a book at speeds that could be adjusted from 200 to more than 2000 words per minute. Another device was moving film, or rather a series of films of printed matter, with the first film scrolling the words over the screen at, say, 200 words per minute, and the tenth film at 500 words per minute.

Positive results came from using any or all of these mechanical motivational devices. And then it was discovered that a book like *Reading Skills* could provide dramatic successes without using any mechanical devices except a wristwatch.

In a regular organized reading program with a dozen people or more, the mechanical devices are practical and clearly motivational. But what if you are using *Reading Skills* on your own? Are there mechanical devices you can turn to? The answer is yes, if you have a personal computer. I'll try to explain how you can use a computer to increase your reading speed. I'll also try to make clear the limitations.

Most of the personal computers have a software program that allows one to scroll the material up the screen, just as do the motivational speed-reading films. The scrolling effect is more jerky than the sixteen-millimeter films, but the intensity of the motivation is exactly the same. Each software program may offer different rates of scrolling speed, but I will illustrate the principle by citing the program on my machine, Wordstar. Using the first thousand-word chapter of *Reading Skills* and using the index to my computer manual, which told me quickly how to enter the scrolling mode, I experimented on myself, and I found that once the computer is scrolling, it is possible to vary the rate of words moving up the screen on a scale from one to five, with five the lowest practical speed for a reading program. I soon became immersed in the game and motivated my tired old bones to get moving.

At the fastest speed (1) the scroller zipped the material over the screen at 2000 words per minute. At the next slower speed (2) the material scrolled at 1000 words per minute. At the "normal" speed (3) the rate was 570 words per minute. At the next (4) it was 300 words per minute, and at the slowest (5) it was 150 words per minute, or slow enough to read aloud. I had to accustom myself to the jerk every time a line of print moved, but I found it wasn't a major handicap, and after three or four lines I was quite adjusted to the mechanics.

Of course not everyone has a personal computer, and the chief difficulty in using one for improving reading speed is that you don't ordinarily have a thousand-word item on your floppy disc. These two objections aside, the principle is sound, and it may be something of an adventure to work with another person, exchange floppy discs with a counted number of words (personal computers usually have a way of counting—on my software I simply use the Spellstar program for word counting), and start scrolling slightly faster than your "normal" rate. You will need to push yourself to keep up, but that's what a speed-reading program is all about. It will seem as if the moving lines on the screen are pushing you. The process will teach you to concentrate more intensively than you thought possible. You are likely to be surprised at how much you can take in at what will seem fantastic rates.

The sixteen-millimeter films scroll at rates that increase on the order of fifty words per minute for each film, enabling you to sense that you are gradually but definitely increasing your reading rate. The personal computer does not allow such a gradual increase, so that if you begin at the setting that scrolls at 300 words per minute, you are forced to make a fairly drastic jump to 570 words per minute when you move on to the next faster setting. Never mind. The effort to keep up will motivate you all the more, and the sense of pushing and pushing is, after all, the chief method you use to teach yourself to read faster.

Several attempts at the 570 rate will be discouraging if you can't keep up. Therefore, it would be best to use the chapters of this book until you can come near the 570 rate, say 470 words per minute, and then try the scrolling technique. Give yourself something high to aim at, but anything more that a 100-word-per-minute increase is probably too much to attempt at once.

One important caution. You can't expect to read as fast off the machine, at least not at first. You need to practice your "machine-increased" rate of reading as soon as you finish using the machine, and it would be a good idea to do it immediately. Even a half-hour delay will probably have a negative effect on your increased speed. Using material that is easily timed, such as the next chapter of *Reading Skills*, test your new rate to see if it matches the speed you reached on the machine. And as in all skill programs, you need to put into practice daily the techniques and principles you are learning. The machine can only give you a good, solid push.

Many thousands have increased their speed of reading without using mechanical devices, but the motivational impact of new machines that are as widely used as typewriters were some years ago is not to be denied. Think of it as a game and accept the challenge of showing that humans are superior to machines.

Record your rate here: _____
Average rate for Chapter 9: 390 wpm. Turn to the Comprehension
Check on page 118.

Application Exercise: Chapter 9

Promising Yourself Rewards

Motivation is the key to better performance. The word means "a stimulus to action" or "something that provides you an incentive." An obvious motivation comes from using a mechanical device, such as a computer, to increase reading rate, a suggestion mentioned in the previous chapter. But if you don't have one, you can at least probe into how deep your motivation is to read more effectively. Answering the following questions will get you started on a list of promises to yourself:

1. What motivated you to begin a program of rapid reading?
2. Have you made progress in rate since you began? How much?
3. Do you record your rate after reading each chapter?
4. Is your motivation sufficient to read a chapter a day or three a week? If not, can you say why?
5. Is an increase in rate a sufficient reward? Do you need other kinds of rewards to motivate you, such as praise from another? What other rewards would motivate you?
6. Theoretically if your rate improves, you can read more material. Are you reading more? Cite an example.
7. Are you keeping a list of things you want to read when you fulfill the expectations of this program? Jot down a few.
8. What are your expectations of the rate part of this program?
9. Often reinforcement comes from the encouragement of friends and acquaintances. Have you told others of your interest in this program? What kinds of responses did you get?
10. The reading program you are engaged in calls for more than rate improvement. Are you doing a better job of figuring out the meaning of words as they appear in context? Are you adding to your vocabulary? List a few words new to you.
11. Do you have a better understanding of how to find the main idea of a paragraph or essay?
12. Are you taking the Comprehension Check after the timed readings? Are you scoring well on the checks?
13. Does pushing to increase your rate help you to concentrate more effectively? If your concentration wanders occasionally, can you say why?
14. Have you applied your increased reading skill to material other than this text? Cite instances.
15. Have you made an attempt to organize your schedule so you have more time for reading? Illustrate.
16. Is it possible to further reorganize your schedule? How?
17. Do you have time for light reading? Illustrate.
18. Are you trying to improve your memory? If so, without looking back, do you remember who wrote the item on the stream of consciousness?

19. Do you consciously shift gears (change rates) when you move from difficult to easy material? Illustrate.
20. When was the last time you used your skills in skimming material? List the material you skimmed.
21. In addition to reading more rapidly, what are your other reading goals? List two or three.

10 *Forming Habits*

Ignoring for a moment the methods used to teach you reading when you were a child (think and say? phonics? phonetics? double combinations?), after the first halting year or two you were on your own. You progressed at your own rate, and under guidance you gradually increased your rate until you could read aloud without hesitating. The chances are you were not taught how to increase your rate beyond that point, but there is nothing sacred about that rate, is there? Isn't it simply a habit you can change?

How are one's habits formed? Psychologists do not know exactly, but agree that habits have something to do with the nervous system. The assumption is that a stimulus, let us say the sight of a printed word, begins a nervous impulse that, starting through the eye, runs its course to the brain. The impulse, finding its way by some route through the nerve cells, leaves a path that offers less resistance to the next impulse. When the next impulse is started, it makes the path still easier to travel, so that succeeding impulses follow the path very readily, finally even automatically. Thus a habit is formed.

You may ask what determines the path of the original nerve impulse to the brain. Again, no one knows exactly, but once that path begins to get worn, unless there is a good reason for changing the path, you will keep it. You have acquired certain reading habits, and unless you are convinced that there are better habits, you will keep the ones you have.

Consider what habits do for us. They direct our movements and lessen fatigue. Watch children who are learning to tie shoelaces, and you will see the value of habits. If movements did not become automatic through practice, it would be continually necessary to repeat the child's trial-and-error method. Habits lessen fatigue because the nervous system tends to do things in the simplest possible way, the way that requires the least energy. Therefore, once we find an easy way of doing something, we conserve energy by establishing this easy way as a habit.

Because our habits make our movements automatic, they first reduce and then eliminate the need to pay attention to the performance of various acts. Consider how difficult it would be to pay attention to everything we do when we operate a car. When we are learning to drive, we must think about turning on the ignition, pushing in the clutch and shifting the gears (unless the car has an automatic shift), and regulating the gas. If we had to continue concentrating on each mechanical aspect of driving, we would be poor drivers indeed. Fortunately, habit takes over, and we soon find ourselves paying more attention to other drivers, which is as it should be.

But though habits are useful things, they also present a serious difficulty. Practice, we are told, makes perfect; but, as someone has remarked, it would be truer to say that practice makes permanent. If you are a word-by-word reader and you repeat the practice until it becomes firmly ingrained, you are in the unfortunate position of possessing a habit you would be far better off without—one that you will not banish until, through practice and discipline, you acquire another habit to replace it.

In order to possess good reading habits you must consciously set about acquiring some and avoiding others. You should, for example, attempt to form the habits of concentrating intensively and of seeing words in groups, but you should avoid, as we have said before, allowing yourself to fall into the habit of a single reading speed for all kinds of material.

Forming good reading habits is fairly simple if one really has the desire to do so. Let us consider the situation for typical readers, who wanted to learn to read faster. They were average readers when they started their period of training, which means that their speed was about 300 words per minute. During the first few days of training they showed a gradual but definite increase, and about the tenth or twelfth day there was a considerable jump in speed. Then the increase was gradual again until the eighteenth or twentieth day, when the speed began to level off to about 800 words per minute. It might have been possible for them to increase their speed even more, but the chances are that a significant increase from that point would take two or three times as long to achieve. They were satisfied with their newly acquired rate of reading and had little desire to improve any more; for this reason it would take longer now to increase their speed.

If their daily rate of reading was plotted on a chart, the line would resemble a curve that ascended gradually as if they were climbing a hill and then leveled off as if they had reached a plateau at the top of the hill. The gradual increase in the beginning might be attributed to their difficulty in overcoming old habits of reading, and the jump halfway through the twenty periods of practice probably would represent their final throwing off of these old habits and their acquiring of the new. Had they stopped practicing after the tenth period, it is quite probable that they soon would have reverted to the old habits. Since they continued to work, however, they were able to give the new habits a chance to become automatic. And by the time they had practiced reading at the increased speed for six or eight periods, the new habits were just about as automatic as the old ones used to be.

The twenty-four chapters of *Reading Skills* offer plenty of opportunity to form new habits.

Not all readers are exactly alike, of course, but many follow a similar pattern of learning in their attempt to increase reading speed. The thing to remember is that readers with a strong desire to better their speed will practice regularly, and they will not give up until they are satisfied that their new habits have become automatic.

Record your rate here: _____

Average rate for Chapter 10: 400 wpm. Turn to the Comprehension Check on page 119.

Application Exercise: Chapter 10

Checking for Changes

If you followed the suggestions in Chapter 2, you checked your reading habits when you started this book. Now, to see if your reading habits have changed since you began this program, answer the questions below.

1. Have you been able to identify reading habits that keep your speed down? If so, name them.
2. Have your study habits changed as a result of a deliberate attempt to do so? Without consulting your schedule, can you say how many hours a week you really study? How many hours do you spend on recreational reading? If you need to check your schedule, do so.
3. What is the one reading or study habit you would improve if you could just wave a magic wand?
4. Since magic wands are in short supply, what plan have you worked out to improve the one habit you listed in item 3?
5. How much of a difference in rate is there now in your reading of difficult and easy material? Rate on difficult material: _____. Rate on easy material: _____.
6. Is there a noticeable difference now in the amount of material you read per week? Are you attacking your study program with more confidence?
7. Have you established a favorite place to do your reading?
8. Can you remember what you read more easily? the same?
9. Can you now enjoy reading more? the same?
10. Do you feel your overall reading efficiency has changed? Explain in a sentence or two why you think it has (or has not).

Note: If you feel there has been no improvement in your reading habits since you began this program, you should probably work to improve your own motivation (promise yourself a better reward).

Vocabulary in Context II

The words below have been selected from the Application Exercises for Chapters 5, 6, and 8. Match the words with their definitions by writing the number of the word next to its definition. The Answer Key is on page 134.

Words from Chapter 5

1. disposition
2. marshaling
3. sloth
4. affection
5. humor
6. pruning
7. confute
8. wit
9. impediment
10. wrought out

_____ state of mind
_____ worked out
_____ block
_____ temperament
_____ cutting overgrowth
_____ pretence
_____ bringing together
_____ lively intelligence
_____ laziness
_____ speak against

Words from Chapter 6

1. extract
2. metabolism
3. titular
4. alma mater
5. restitution
6. reparation

_____ one's school
_____ compensation for damage
_____ isolated substance
_____ bodily process
_____ bearing a title
_____ amends

Words from Chapter 8

1. cyclical
2. forlorn
3. impressionistic
4. pervert
5. squalid
6. epic

_____ designating grandeur and sweep
_____ to corrupt or debase
_____ sordid, indecent
_____ wretched; nearly hopeless
_____ characterized by the use of details and mental associations to evoke a subjective view rather than reality
_____ relating to a repeated sequence of events

11 *Getting Inside the System*

When authors attempt to transmit information about almost any kind of system, they use at least two codes. The first is the English language, if, of course, the audience of intended readers speaks English. Language is a systematic collection of symbols representing the sounds we use to convey meaning. The second code is a plan of organization that can often be reduced to an outline or at least to a skeleton where the bones or structure are apparent. The second code uses mechanical aids, to be discussed here.

Authors of textbooks, technical manuals, and works of nonfiction want their readers to see the structure of the body of information they are trying to transmit. For this reason they will advertise their code to make the bones of the structure stand out. In this book, for example, one of the elements of structure is the division of the text into twenty-four chapters. Another is the division of each chapter into two parts: a timed reading exercise such as the one you are reading now, and an Application Exercise.

"Mechanical aids" refers to such things as different sizes and kinds of type and to punctuation marks—the various signals that serve as road signs, so to speak, and that guide readers to the author's meaning. Modern writers of fiction are acutely aware of these special devices in reading. In books like Virginia Woolf's *The Waves* or Tillie Olsen's *Tell Me a Riddle*, the reader must understand what the author is trying to do with unusual typographical devices. Whole sections are printed in italics, for example, to show that they exist in the minds of the characters or are not expressed aloud. Some authors use italics to show dream states or to suggest a stream of consciousness.

The mechanical aids used by Woolf, Olsen, and other modern authors are more than matched by the people who write textbooks. Some aids in textbooks—such as titles, chapter headings, and subheadings, each in its own distinctive type—are obvious. Others are not too plain, for example, special words like *however, moreover,* or *nevertheless* that refer to ideas that have come before or will come after, or words like *primarily, chiefly,* or *especially,* used to stress the value of important points. These will be discussed shortly.

Modern techniques of printing allow a wide variation of sizes and shapes of type. The use of boldface, italics, and capitals is very important. Boldface is thick, heavy type that is used for emphasis. **Boldface looks like this**. Boldface printing is usually used for chapter titles and directions. Italics are also used for emphasis; they are different from boldface in that the lines are thin, slope to the right, and are made to look like handwriting. *Italics look like this.* They often stress special words or indicate the pitch of a word. Titles are usually printed in italic type. For very strong emphasis, CAPITAL LETTERS are sometimes used.

Various other devices, such as the method of punctuating, serve very well to draw your attention to an author's meaning. Quotation marks around words, for example, mean that the author intends to put special stress on these words. Setting off a phrase with a dash or with parentheses often means to imply that these phrases are "by-the-way" remarks or afterthoughts. Such punctuation marks as the exclamation point, question mark, colon, and semicolon all have specific uses. If you are uncertain about what any of them means, study a manual of usage so that you are familiar with how to use them. To make the author's meaning clearer, pictures, charts, and diagrams are often used where words by themselves would fail.

But those who write textbooks must, of course, rely mainly on a good choice of words to convey their ideas. The Chinese proverb, "A picture is worth a thousand words," and the modern adaptation, "The right word wisely chosen is worth ten thousand carelessly chosen words," are equally true. At any rate, it is with words that we deal most as readers, and certain of them deserve special mention. Words to show contrast, like *however* or *yet*, keep guiding the reader to the author's meaning. Reference words and phrases, such as *this, that, these*, and *those*, like the contrast words, relate one part of the sentence to another. Words like *moreover, further*, and *besides* tell us to look for something more. Phrases that contain numbers (*two* ways, *five* points) tell us how the thought is to be set up, and words like *in particular* and *especially* are often used to indicate a main point.

An outline is often used to show how a subject is to be treated. Subdivided under numbers or letters, the main elements in the argument stand apart from each other and are distinct. Usually main ideas are set off by Roman numerals, and minor ideas by capital letters, Arabic numerals, and lower-case letters. The outline is a display, clear and concise, of the main points of the text. Whenever authors provide one, you will find it a great help in quickly understanding their system.

Generally speaking, authors of textbooks or technical manuals are working to provide a clear code for the reader, and copy editors are checking to see that the code is discernible. If we could get into the minds of authors, we would see that they try to show and tell, revealing step-by-step processes. Usually their efforts pay off.

If a text is not outlined in an obvious way, all you need to do is examine the order of the paragraphs to see how the author divides ideas. In well-written text you can often get a fairly good idea of the author's purpose by reading the first and last paragraphs of a chapter or section, because good writers usually will tell you where they are going and where they have been.

As your object in reading is to find the writer's complete meaning, you should examine the ways authors mark what they have to say. To neglect these ways is to fly blind.

Record your rate here: _____
Average rate for Chapter 11: 415 wpm. Turn to the Comprehension Check on page 120.

Application Exercise: Chapter 11

Taking Exams

Objective Exams

Professors with classes of over thirty students often turn to the objective examination as a means of measuring ability. Many professors feel that an objective (1) can get at the heart of the matter more precisely than an essay and that (2) it does a fairer and clearer job of distinguishing between good and poor students. Also, (3) the mechanics of taking an objective exam are relatively easy and (4) students are tested for what they actually know, not for how well they can express it.

There is a sound method of taking an objective examination that eliminates almost every possibility of getting tangled with mechanics. *The method has five steps. First,* read the directions carefully and allot your time in proportion to the weighting of the questions. *Second,* go through all the questions and answer only those you are positive you know. *Third,* go through the list again and answer those you are reasonably sure of. *Fourth,* work on the questions that stump you, making a careful guess rather than leaving a blank. *Fifth,* review all the questions and make changes only if you are positive that the first answer was incorrect.

Essay Exams

The key to writing a good essay exam is a careful reading of directions. Match the meanings with the words below by placing the number of the correct word in the blank:

1. analyze
2. characterize
3. compare
4. contrast
5. discuss
6. explain
7. illustrate
8. summarize

_____ 1. to describe the qualities or pecularities of
_____ 2. to restate briefly or in condensed form
_____ 3. to set in opposition in order to show or emphasize differences.
_____ 4. to make plain or comprehensible; to define; explicate; expound, to offer reasons for.
_____ 5. to examine in order to note similarities or differences.
_____ 6. to examine a subject closely with a view to interchanging opinions.
_____ 7. to clarify by use of examples or comparisons
_____ 8. to separate into parts or basic principles so as to determine the nature of the whole.

Answer Key is found on page 135.

Preparing for an Exam

When I was in graduate school I took a course in American history from a man who was an excellent teacher but a stiff marker. Here's how I prepared for the final exam. (1) I took careful and systematic notes at the daily lectures, trying to get everything into them: general statements, relationships, and important principles;

51

but I concentrated most on getting (a) names, (b) dates, (c) publications, (d) places, and (e) examples. Fortunately I had a free hour following lectures so (2) I went to my desk and worked over notes right away. (3) I looked up the names, dates, and publications in my reference books, trying to find out more about them so they would stick in my mind. At the end of the week, (4) I typed up the lecture notes and reviewed them with a red pencil in hand. Then (5) several times during the course I typed notes from assigned readings and correlated them with the lecture notes. Where the teacher had mentioned one fact or example to back up a generalization, I tried to supplement it with as many as I could find from the readings. When it came time for the final review, (6) I assembled all of my summaries and studied them. During the last week, (7) I went to the library and asked for the past exams that had been put on file for that course. I didn't worry about answering the old questions but rather concerned myself with the type of material the questions seemed to search for. Then (8) *I made out my own exam and carefully prepared the answers.* That final week (9) I spent one period a day in review and (10) I went to bed early the night before the exam, confident that I had learned enough about one period of American history to write a textbook if need be.

The exam was a fair one, and my only problem was selecting the best facts and examples to write down. P. S. I passed.

Open-book quiz. On a separate sheet:

1. List the five steps in taking an objective exam.
2. List the ten steps the author took to prepare for an essay exam.
3. List nine key words in essay exams.

Key Abbreviations

One type of word signal that can easily be classified and learned is the frequently used abbreviation. An example is *e.g.* It means *for example*. If you look up the meaning of the following frequently used abbreviations, you won't have to puzzle over them the next time they turn up in your reading:

1. *i.e.*
2. *cf.*
3. *passim.*
4. *etc.*
5. *bf.*
6. *et al.*
7. *do.*
8. *ff.*
9. *viz.*

12 *Relating to Meaning*

Your ability to comprehend and critically evaluate what you read depends on your knowing the meaning of a large number of the words you see in print. A person who reads well at the adult level must inevitably possess a sizable vocabulary.

You can enrich your vocabulary in various ways, but perhaps the best way is through your ordinary reading. There is good reason why this is a better way than studying word lists as many people do. A word standing by itself in a list does not offer clues to its meaning as does a word used in a sentence. You can learn about an unknown word in *context* by relating it to the meaning of the words that surround it. Take, for example, the work *context*. You can easily arrive at its meaning by noting the words around it. You note also that these surrounding words *relate to it in meaning*. Thus you have discovered that *context* means "surrounding words that are directly connected to a given word and that add to its meaning."

Learning words in context is, as we have said, the best and often the easiest way to improve your vocabulary. But no matter how true this may generally be, you will find that you are frequently led to the dictionary. The habit of using the dictionary is absolutely necessary for a person who expects to have a rich and varied vocabulary. Browse occasionally in a good dictionary. Believe it or not, your dictionary can provide many an evening of diversion that will pay valuable dividends.

The dictionary will usually offer a choice of several meanings for a word, allowing the reader to select the meaning that is best in each circumstance. First try to determine its meaning from the way it is used in your reading; then check your work with the dictionary.

However, you should not overlook words that come to you from sources other than reading. Do not hesitate to stop someone who uses a word you do not know and ask what it means. This may seem embarrassing, but you will find that nine times out of ten the person will respect you for asking. And it is better than making a wrong guess about a word's meaning. In fact a hazy notion of a word meaning may be less helpful than none at all. Hucksters and "confidence men," and even some unscrupulous politicians, try to confuse the public by using words that mean one thing but sound like something else. A senator who was running for re-election was accused by his opponents of deliberately living a life of celibacy before marriage. The voters evidently listened to the words "accused" and "deliberately" and felt that the key word to follow would be unfavorable to the senator. When they heard "celibacy" followed by "before marriage" they were misled into thinking the senator was a scoundrel and he was not re-elected. His opponents guessed that very few would know that the exact meaning of celibacy was an "unmarried state," and they fooled those who make a habit of settling for a hazy notion of a word meaning.

A good stock of exact meanings will give you a distinct advantage in reading, for you will be able to comment on authors more intelligently. Learn to test the value of an author's choice of words and challenge those choices at every step taken to mold a reader's opinion. It is not enough to have a good vocabulary. It is not enough to understand. It is important to use your understanding of word meanings as a *tool of criticism*. Become aware of words used like a broadsword to drive home points emotionally in contrast to those used as a rapier, making deft, rational thrusts at the reader's mind. Two examples will point up the difference between the two techniques, and both will serve to show that it is not necessary to use five-syllable words to say something profound or moving.

In 1862 Abraham Lincoln wrote to Horace Greeley that he did not want his war policy to be in doubt. Note the rapier simplicity of language, the parallel constructions, and the appeal mainly to one's reason. "My paramount object in this struggle is to save the Union, and is not either to save or to destroy slavery. If I could save the Union without freeing any slave, I would do it; and if I could save it by freeing all the slaves, I would do it; and if I could save it by freeing some and leaving others alone, I would also do that. What I do about slavery and the coloured race, I do because I believe it helps to save the Union; and what I forbear, I forbear because I do not believe it would help to save the Union. I shall do less whenever I shall believe what I am doing hurts the cause, and I shall do more whenever I shall believe doing more will help the cause. I shall try to correct errors when shown to be errors, and I shall adopt new views so fast as they shall appear to be true views."

And here are words used as a smashing broadsword with a strong appeal to emotions. Patrick Henry said, "Gentlemen may cry peace, peace—but there is no peace. The war is actually begun! The next gale that sweeps from the north will bring to our ears the clash of resounding arms! Our brethren are already in the field! Why stand we here idle? What is it that gentlemen wish? What would they have? Is life so dear, or peace so sweet, as to be purchased at the price of chains and slavery? Forbid it, Almighty God! I know not what course others may take; but as for me, give me liberty, or give me death!"

Using your understanding of word meanings is as important as the size of your vocabulary. An important basis for judging people ought not to be their current level of achievement, but rather how actively they are taking steps to better themselves. Develop a real curiosity about words and you have taken a great stride toward successful reading.

Average rate for Chapter 12: 415 wpm. Turn to the Comprehension Check on page 121.

Application Exercise: Chapter 12

Scrutinizing Shades of Meaning

Synonyms are words with meanings that are similar but seldom precisely the same—there is almost always a different shade to the meaning. Using the exact shade of meaning is every author's aim. "The difference between the exact word and almost the exact word," said Mark Twain, "is the difference between lightning and the lightning bug." Synonyms are often listed in such desk references as *The American Heritage Dictionary*, which was used to devise the list below. While the words themselves are not defined, the different shades of meaning are explained. To alert yourself to shades of meaning among synonyms, complete the following exercises by filling in the blank with the correct word (see Answer Key on page 135 for correct responses):

1. *Awkward* implies lack of grace in movement, often interchangeable with *clumsy*, although *clumsy* emphasizes lack of dexterity in movement; *maladroit* implies lack of skill with other persons, while *inept* applies to inappropriate actions and speech; *gauche* suggests boorishness, and *bungling* implies gross incompetence in performance.
   * On the stage she missed her lines and wandered about, drawing the criticism that she was _____.
2. *Conflict* applies to a large-scale struggle or a struggle within a person; *contest* can mean either friendly competition or a struggle between hostile forces; *fight* usually means a clash involving two persons or a small group, or a struggle for a cause; *affray, melee, and scuffle* all denote impromptu and disorderly clashes.
   * There was a _____ in the ring between two boxers.
3. *Dead* is a general term meaning that what was once alive is no longer; *deceased* refers only to humans, as does *departed* (a euphemism); *extinct* means there are no living successors (animals or a volcano); *lifeless* means no longer alive or without spirit; *inanimate* means it never was alive.
   * The dodo bird is said to be _____.
4. *Incite* means arousing the will and spirit to act, as by forceful oratory; *instigate* means conceiving a plan of action, often drastic, and making it work; *foment* means systematically arousing discord, rebellion, or the like, which produce violent action; *abet* means active aid or tacit approval of actions, especially against what is right or proper.
   * Patrick Henry's words helped to _____ his countrymen.
5. *Include* and *comprise* both take as objects things that are part of something larger; *comprise* additionally means all of the parts are stated; *comprehend* and *embrace* mean taking in of intangibles as part of a broader subject; *involve* means a relationship of a thing that is a logical consequence of something more inclusive.
   * Heavy work schedules _____ extra effort.
6. *Obligation* means an immediate and defined constraint in conduct (as in a contract or treaty); *responsibility* means in a more general way that for

which one is accountable; *duty* means conduct which comes from moral or ethical considerations.

- Patriotic citizens have a _____ to serve their country.

7. *Obstacle* applies to what must be removed, circumvented, or surmounted; *obstruction* means physical interference with passage; *bar* and *barrier* stress difficulty of passage to the point of implying prohibition; *block* means equally strong opposition of a more temporary duration; *impediment* means interference with normal function but not cessation of function; *hindrance* implies mere delay; *encumbrance* applies to that which weighs down; *snag* means unforeseen and usually transitory opposition.

- Yesterday the delegates encountered a _____ that they did not expect and they hope to surmount it today.

8. *Phase* means a stage or period of development as a temporary attitude or manner; *aspect* means a single area of interest; a *facet* means one of several aspects of a problem; *angle* means a deliberate limitation of perspective, with emphasis on the observer's view; *side* means discussion of an issue over which opinion has been divided into two points of view.

- A teenager is going through a new _____ of life.

9. *Reveal* means to make known what was secret; *expose* means to make public that which was reprehensible, such as a crime; *disclose* means to make known something that has been kept from the public; *divulge* means making known what was known to a small circle as a secret; *impart* means to share knowledge with another; *betray* means making known and thereby breaking a trust.

- A political candidate will sometimes _____ his rival to gain advantage.

10. *Series* means like or related things arranged in order; *succession* means arranged in order of time and without interruption; *progression* reveals a definite pattern of advance; *sequence* means an order in causal or logical relationship; *chain* means a closely linked sequence; *train* means a procession of persons or vehicles or a sequence of ideas or events; *string* means a continuous succession.

- She was fifth in line of _____ to the throne.

11. *Ultimate* applies to that which terminates a lengthy progression with nothing after it; *last* applies to that which brings a series of like things to an end; *final* stresses the definiteness of the conclusion; *terminal* applies to that which marks a limit in space, time, or development; *eventual* refers to an outcome or issue, and sometimes it implies a foreseeable or inevitable result.

- The cancerous growth was in the _____ stage.

12. *Work* can refer not only to the effort of persons but also to the activity of machines and the forces of nature; *labor* refers mostly to human effort; *toil* refers to strenuous and fatiguing labor; *drudgery* refers to dull, wearisome, monotonous, and sometimes demeaning labor; *travail* means work involving great effort and pain or suffering.

- Sanding welded joints on the automotive assembly line for ten years is _____.

13 *Taking Notes*

Particularly when you are studying, the taking of notes is a valuable means of increasing reading efficiency. To be sure, taking notes will slow down your reading speed; on the other hand, it will force you to read more carefully.

Books are fine things, but they are not as sacred as some people think them to be. The familiar childhood command, "Do not write in books!" is so thoroughly drilled into some people that they feel a twinge of guilt whenever they are tempted to write in the margin. Certainly we shouldn't write in books that do not belong to us, but for your own books the command should be forgotten. In fact, many people feel that a book becomes more valuable to them if they do write in it. Furthermore, if the notes that are written in a book are intelligent ones, other readers of the book will benefit as well.

As illustrated here, a good way to begin is to <u>underline significant statements</u> What is a significant statement? It is often one upon which all the others depend, as the branches of a tree depend on a trunk. The test? If you omit a significant (or leading, or main, or central) statement, those that follow will fail to fit—that is, they will have nothing to relate to.

Some readers find it a good practice to underline in red a certain type of key statement, for example, the central idea of a chapter or section. They then underline the subordinate ideas in blue and significant illustrations in black. If there is too much that seems to need underlining, perhaps you will want to jot down in the margin a statement of your own, summarizing a particular paragraph or section. Again you might use different colored pencils to show different types of material.

When you use a multicolor system you can review the book easily and in several ways. You can flip through the pages, glancing only at those passages in red to find the central ideas, or you can be more thorough in your review and note the blue-penciled subordinate ideas and perhaps the black-penciled illustrative passages as well. People who use this method say it helps them to see things clearly and quickly.

Notes in the margin—for example, a clear phrasing of a topic idea or a comment of your own reaction to what you've read—may also be valuable. If your reading brings up a question that the author fails to answer, jot it down in the proper place in the margin. When you come to evaluating the book, such questions will be helpful.

Another method of note taking has gained popularity with the almost universal presence of the tape recorder. The act of speaking the words into the recorder forces them into your memory in a way that reading silently cannot match. Using the tape recorder for notes is also helpful when you are doing newspaper or magazine research in the library and do not have access to a photocopying machine. It may be necessary to type up the notes once you are in your accustomed study space, but the triple method of taking notes (voice, eye, and hand) will help fix the material in your mind. Recording a lecture does not provide an active grappling with the material.

For those of us who haven't learned shorthand, an improvised system of abbreviations often works well enough. Titles of books or stories can be written with initials or one word; thus, Virginia Woolf's *A Room of One's Own* becomes "W's 'Room,'" and Hawthorne's *The Scarlet Letter* becomes "H's 'SL'." In abbreviated language, "The importance of the economic and political analysis of the Declaration of Independence," becomes "t impt of t ec & pol anal of t Decl of Ind." The idea is to devise your own shorthand system.

An impt pt in note taking is to watch for summaries, conclusions, and recapitulations, for the meat and logic of the material is found there. If you find a way of arguing with a conclusion, you stand a better chance of remembering it—which is the purpose of note taking in the first place.

Respect for the property of others will haunt your conscience if you mark in library books. It is always discouraging to come upon a library book someone has thoughtlessly marked and messed up. A good method of note taking if the book is not your own is to use a large note card, making an index of items to return to later.

Taking notes on the standard 3-by-5-inch or 4-by-6-inch cards has several advantages. It is usually desirable to take notes and arrange them according to subject headings rather than according to sources. This procedure can of course be adapted to a computer with a capacity for indexing, allowing for a printout as flexible as the card system.

A standard procedure is to write the subject of the card, say, "Iran Controversy," in the upper right-hand corner and the author and title of the book in the upper left-hand corner. When you do this you can file the card by subject, author, or title. Don't be stingy with your cards; they will be most helpful to you if they represent fairly narrow divisions of your subject. Your aim should be to have cards that you can shuffle and arrange to suit a variety of purposes.

Note taking, like reading, can be done more efficiently if you do it with a special purpose in mind. The form of your notes should also be adapted to suit your purpose. An outline, for example, will help you to keep in mind the main ideas of the book and will help you remember the relation of the ideas. On the other hand, a summary—in your own words—will be easier to read, and perhaps a little more satisfactory for review. A good general rule is to quote the authors only if they put the statement in a memorable way or if you know in advance that you will have a special use for the quotation. In most cases those notes in which you summarize material in your own words will be more useful to you.

Average rate on Chapter 13: 430 wpm. Turn to the Comprehension
Check on page 122.

Application Exercise: Chapter 13

Using Your Own Words

A good note taker constantly fights against the impulse to copy the reading instead
of taking notes on it. The idea is to remember what you have read; furthermore, in
this day of the copy machine, it is not necessary to transfer blocks of material from a
text to your notes. Use the machine if you need to copy pages. Note taking, on the
other hand, is an opportunity to think out material as you read and to restate it in
your own words.

Make brief and condensed notes of the following 500-word essay on Gertrude
Stein, an exercise I wrote many years ago.

Copies of the "word portrait" of the art patron, Mabel Dodge,
Gertrude Stein's hostess in Florence in August, 1912, were bound in
assorted Florentine wallpapers and distributed to Mabel Dodge's friends;
about six months later Mabel Dodge arranged its publication in the issue
of *Arts and Decoration* devoted to the Cubist exhibition at the 69th
Regiment Armory in New York, an exhibit described as "the Great Event
in the history of American Art." When the Cubists' exhibit burst like a
cultural starshell on the American art scene (over one hundred thousand
people came to see it the first month), some of its "radiance by association" was enjoyed by Gertrude Stein, all the more welcome because she
was having trouble getting published.

In a characteristic shout of enthusiasm Mabel Dodge wrote, "You
are just on the eve of bursting. . . . Everywhere I go [people are] talking
of Gertrude Stein," and Gertrude Stein replied, "Hooray for *gloire.*"

At thirty-nine Gertrude Stein was finally getting reinforcement for
her experimental writing. As Mabel Dodge wrote in 1936, "This was the
first time the public . . . had heard of Gertrude Stein. . . . From that year,
when her essence was poured into the public consciousness, she has crept
through it like a slow, inevitable tincture."

Ironically, the portrait that brought Gertrude Stein to the attention
of the intelligentsia in 1913 has not been decoded. Other than Mabel
Dodge herself no one has pushed beneath the surface to find the hidden
meaning. As an experiment in stream-of-consciousness writing, it was
not entirely successful. And although it did break a pathway, it was
nevertheless an early attempt practiced by an author who was trying to
carve out a theory at the same time she created the work of art. She knew
her creation was ugly. "In struggling away from [the persistent drag of
habits]" she said, "there is always an ugliness. . . . But the essence of that
ugliness is the thing which will always make it beautiful. I myself think it

is much more interesting when it seems ugly, because in it you see the element of the fight."

A great part of the portrait is unintelligible, but what people don't understand, they either reject or revere. The association of this portrait with the Armory Show gave it an aura if not of reverence then at least of being "in." As Desmond MacCarthy said of Gertrude Stein's work in 1932, the threat of being called a philistine "has an alarming effect upon people in whom the desire to be right about art is rather stronger than their power to enjoy it."

There is no doubt that she was aware that she was unintelligible. Her response to a publisher's request for "the comprehensible thing, the thing the public can understand," was, "My work would have been no use to anyone if the public had understood me early and first." Donald Sutherland, perhaps her most perceptive biographer, writing in 1951 said, "Gertrude Stein can be thought of as a thoroughly civilized woman operating in Indian territory. . . . As more and more people go over the same ground, her work will seem more natural."

Making Your Own Index

On a separate paper, make your own index of those topics in this book up to Chapter 13 that interest you most. Other possibilities for an index are: authors of books, book titles, anecdotes about authors.

An effective way of alphabetizing an index of more than 100 items is to write each entry and its page number on a roll of adding machine paper, cutting off each entry with a scissors, spreading the individual entries on a table to place them in rough alphabetical order, and finally sorting them in exact order before writing them in a list. Of course, if the program for your personal computer has alphabetizing capabilities, the task is that much simpler.

14 *Summarizing*

In a previous chapter you read that Bacon said, "Some books are to be chewed and digested. . . ." For the books that need to be chewed and digested, making a written summary is an effective means to the end.

If, in taking notes on your reading, you put them in summary form *and in your own words*, you will find your notes much more useful to you than if you merely put down an occasional idea that strikes you as important. Such note taking lacks clarity and organization. Your aim should be to have notes that represent, in capsule form, what you have read, and for this the best method is to summarize.

Summarizing forces you to exact comprehension: To do it well you must understand the author's main ideas and their relation to one another; you must record the key points in a connected form; and you must choose an economical and exact method of expression.

The only way to learn summarizing is by practice. Take an article that interests you and write down the topic sentences of each paragraph. When you finish, read what you have written and you will probably find that you have a fair summary of the article. Now add transitions, making the relationship between sentences as clear as you can. Eliminate any unnecessary words. Abbreviate long words where you can and leave out any short ones that do not add to the meaning. Many students develop a personal shorthand for indicating various standard words and logical relationships. It is quite common, for example, to use three dots (.˙.) for "therefore" and an equals sign (=) when two things are equated.

Another help in summarizing is to examine closely the final statement. If the argument there seems clear, you may find it helpful to restate what is said in your own words and add to it whatever is needed to make it most meaningful to you. It is foolish to try to keep in mind all the facts and examples that have been used to prove the point. But it is also foolish to make the mistake of thinking you will remember them all when you reread your own summary later. Include enough facts and examples to be able to reconstruct the line of thought when you review your notes. It is not enough simply to know the conclusion.

Sometimes you will read a whole paragraph or two that will not contain anything worth recording. At other times, almost every sentence will seem crucial to an understanding of the chapter or section you are reading. Although one hesitates to say so, there are people who are overconscientious and get bogged down in unimportant details. Fearful lest they overlook anything, their notes become so detailed as to be self-defeating. With practice and patience you will learn to separate the wheat from the chaff with increasing skill.

The whole process of summarizing implies an ability to make decisions. You have to decide what the author's plan is, how the material has been organized, what the key ideas are, and what material is used merely as example. You will not find the technique of summarizing easy at first because it requires so many decisions. But your efficiency in making summaries, as well as your general reading efficiency, will increase in proportion to the time and effort you spend on perfecting your note-taking technique.

Your final summary should reflect clearly and accurately what the author has said. An inaccurate summary may be worse than no summary at all. An effective method of testing the quality of your summary is to set it aside for a month or two and then reread it. If it still recalls the essential information for you and seems to express the material in a clear and exact manner, you have done a good job. If it does not, make another attempt. This time you will do a better job. This method, incidentially, may well be applied to other types of writing. Many young writers have been advised to put their material aside for a while. If a piece of writing seems as good a year or two later as the day they finished it, they can begin to feel that it will stand the test of time. The same thing, of course, applies to what someone else has written and you have read. If you think a book you read several years ago was the best you have known, reread it. Don't be surprised if you find yourself sadly disappointed.

Good summaries serve many purposes. Everyone, from professional to houseperson, needs and uses them. Doctors may have to summarize a report of their findings in a particular case for a medical board. They will have to read the summaries of other doctors and summaries of the latest medical research in their field. Lawyers need to prepare a summary, or brief, of their case before they present it in court. Their summary usually takes the form of a sentence outline, and many an early career is hurt by an inability to present a clear and accurate brief. A junior executive may write a summary of a long report for the president of the company. Electrical engineers will summarize their findings to formulate their plans. A student prepares summaries for use in a term paper.

The summary is a convenient and useful tool that saves you time, helps you remember, and lets you see the whole argument at a glance. It should never be regarded as an adequate substitute for reading a book. Once you have read a book, however, a good summary should make it unnecessary for you to spend time reading the book a second time. Though it slows down your reading, summarizing may leave you more time for reading in the long run.

Summary: Summarizing in your own words forces exact comprehension. Examine the final statement, learn to separate unimportant things, decide what the author's plan is, and recall only essential information. A summary saves time, aids the memory, and presents the whole argument.

Record your rate here: _____
Average rate for Chapter 14: 450 wpm. Turn to the Comprehension
Check on page 123.

Application Exercise: Chapter 14

Getting It Together

A forty-word summary is illustrated in the final paragraph of the 1000-word chapter. A good summary condenses the material to a fraction of its original length, and although there is no ideal length, it would be well to aim at something under ten percent of the original.

A good summary:

1. Condenses the original to a fraction of its length;
2. Omits nothing significant, including key examples;
3. Includes only major points;
4. Makes connections (relationships) clear; and
5. Does not distort the original.

Summarize in as few words as possible the following excerpts:

1. From Henry David Thoreau's *Civil Disobedience*: "There will never be a really free and enlightened state until the state comes to recognize the individual as a higher and independent power, from which all its own power and authority are derived, and treats him accordingly. I please myself with imagining a state at last which can afford to be just to all men, and to treat the individual with respect as a neighbor; which even would not think it inconsistent with its own repose if a few were to live aloof from it, not meddling with it, nor embraced by it, who fulfilled all the duties of neighbors and fellow-men. A state which bore this kind of fruit, and suffered it to drop off as fast as it ripened, would prepare the way for a still more perfect and glorious state, which also I have imagined, but not yet anywhere seen."
2. From Abraham Lincoln's *Gettysburg Address* (see Application Exercise for Chapter 19 on page 83).
3. From *The Declaration of Independence* (see Application Exercise for Chapter 1 on page 6).

15 *Using the Library*

Once you have been bitten by the reading bug, you will have an incurable malady. You might as well resign yourself and settle down to a diet of books for the rest of your life. The disease, which is characterized by a voracious reading appetite and an insatiable curiosity about the world of books, can be quite painless if you let it run its natural course and pacify your appetite by reading as often as possible.

Like many other diseases, it can be treated only partially by home remedies—magazines, newspapers, and the books you buy. To combat it successfully, you will have to visit the local library frequently.

Fortunately there are thousands of free libraries about the country, thanks to wise legislators and city administrators, and especially to Andrew Carnegie, who built about 20 percent of our public libraries. The fact that everyone can use these libraries means that, as a whole, Americans have a greater opportunity to read than any other people in the world. Still, all is not as it should be.

Ask an Englishman what Americans are like. He is likely to tell you something like this: "Americans admire bigness and large numbers; they want more of everything; they want things to be stupendous and colossal; they revere the tallest buildings and are awed by huge automobile plants manufacturing thousands of cars a day. Much of the time they worship size for its own sake to the neglect of other important things. They have, for example, more libraries than any other country, but half the people never read a book." Certainly it is never pleasant to listen to someone criticizing our country, but it is difficult not to admit that, in this case at least, truth has been spoken.

It is difficult to believe, but the hard fact is that half the citizens of our country, where nearly everyone can read, do not read one book a year. An investigation of book reading showed that for a three-year period, 48 percent of the people of the United States did not read a book and 18 percent read less than four. That means that over one hundred million Americans did very little or no book reading during one of the most crucial periods in our history. The investigation also showed that over half of the people who didn't read books didn't read magazines either, and sixteen million did not even read the newspaper. This in a nation to which the world looks for enlightened leadership.

If we are to be leaders, we should be readers, although few would argue that all wisdom comes from books and that Americans, therefore, should all rush to their nearest library. Yet it is certainly true that most of our competent leaders are avid readers; to arrive at wise decisions they must be well informed, which means reading widely in many fields.

Most persons who read widely, who devour book after book in search of knowledge and its companion, wisdom, must know how to use the resources of the public library. Let us assume that you are interested in learning about a specific topic and trace your course through the reference system of a library.

The topic in which you are interested is, let us say, Iran's government. You know a little about it, and that little has whetted your appetite. You want to learn more. Your first move, of course, will be to go to the card catalog or one of the library's computer stations. Each book will be listed in three ways in the catalog or on the monitor screen—by subject, author and title. If you cannot remember offhand the author or title of a specific book on Iran's political organization, you can start with the subject listing. There, under the subject of "Iran," you will quite probably find enough books listed to keep you busy for some time. In small libraries you may have to hunt on the shelves for the books you have selected from the catalog. Once you learn the library's system of classification you will be able to do this very easily. In a large library you will simply write the number of the book on a slip of paper, hand it to the librarian at the call desk, and wait until it is delivered to you.

If it happens, as it often does, that the books you read whet your appetite for still more, you will want to return to the library and investigate the magazines. It is not necessary to go rummaging through the back numbers. Consult *The Reader's Guide to Periodical Literature*, an invaluable aid to your reading on just about any subject. Or ask your librarian to assist you by teaching you to do a computer search. In the various recent volumes of *The Reader's Guide*, under the heading of "Iran," you will find the information you need—names of articles and the magazines in which they appear, dates of publication, and so on. *The Reader's Guide* is bound into large volumes annually, but it is also published monthly, so that you can find material in current magazines as well.

Look for the names of magazines that are most likely to suit your purpose, working back through the volumes for a few years or so. *The Atlantic, Harper's* and *The Congressional Digest*, for example, are good magazines to use if you are looking for a reasoned analysis, whereas *Newsweek* or *TV Guide* are more likely to provide a popular treatment of the subject. Most libraries subscribe to these periodicals, and you should have little trouble locating them.

Whether it is magazines or books that you need to consult, keep in mind that a research librarian—or any librarian—will find much satisfaction in helping you get started on your project. Never underestimate the librarian's interest in helping you. And don't be intimidated by thinking that an expert will think you too inexperienced to bother with. The riches of the library are waiting for you. Don't be one of the millions who are strangers to the treasures on its shelves.

Record your rate here: _____

Average rate for Chapter 15: 465 wpm. Turn to the Comprehension Check on page 124.

Application Exercise: Chapter 15

Marking Your X

Here is a short list of reference works available in almost any library. Computer searches have a glamour and can undoubtedly speed things up, but it seems unlikely that they will replace at least a basic knowledge of fundamental tools of the researcher.

Mark an X in front of the items below you are familiar with, and make it your business to find out about the others.

MAGAZINE INDEXES

Applied Science and Technology Index, 1958 to date. For information on engineering journals before 1958, see *Industrial Arts Index.*

Biography Index, 1937 to date. This is a subject index to the biographies in books and journals.

Book Review Digest, 1905 to date. Published book reviews organized by subject, author, and title. Gives excerpts from reviews.

Business Periodicals Index, 1958 to date. Subject listing for business journals.

Education Index, 1929 to date. Subject listing for educational journals, books, and pamphlets.

Humanities Index, 1973 to date. Author and subject listing to humanities journals.

Reader's Guide to Periodical Literature, 1907 to date. Lists articles from several hundred magazines by author and subject. It can give references up to the preceding month.

Social Sciences Index, 1973 to date. Lists author and subject for items in social sciences.

NEWSPAPER INDEXES

The New York Times Index, 1914 to date. Appears monthly. Particularly helpful because it gives the dates of events that were presumably covered in all papers of the same date. Also indexed are *The Christian Science Monitor* and *The Wall Street Journal.*

REFERENCE WORKS—GENERAL

The New Columbia Encyclopedia, 1975. A handy single volume.

Encyclopedia Britannica and *Encyclopedia Americana.* Multivolume sets with annual yearbooks to update material.

Dictionary of National Biography and *Dictionary of American Biography.* Multivolume sets with occasional updates.

Who's Who and *Who's Who In America*. Frequent updates.

World Almanac and Book of Facts. An annual volume.

THE LIBRARY BILL OF RIGHTS

The public library may be the most democratic of American institutions. The list below was adapted by the Council of the American Library Association in 1948, and thereafter by a great many if not most of the public libraries in the country.

Are the policies liberal enough or too liberal? Check those you would want to modify, eliminate, or add to.

1. As a responsibility of library service, books and other library materials selected should be chosen for values of interest, information, and enlightenment of all the people of the community. In no case should library materials be excluded because of the race or nationality or the social, political, or religious views of the authors.

2. Libraries should provide books and other materials presenting all points of view concerning the problems and issues of our times; no library materials should be proscribed or removed from libraries because of partisan or doctrinal disapproval.

3. Censorship should be challenged by libraries in the maintenance of their responsibility to provide public information and enlightenment.

4. Libraries should cooperate with all persons and groups concerned with resisting abridgement of free expression and free access to ideas.

5. The rights of an individual to the use of a library should not be denied or abridged because of his age, race, religion, national origins, or social or political views.

6. As an institution of education for democratic living, the library should welcome the use of its meeting rooms for socially useful and cultural activities and discussion of current public questions. Such meeting places should be available on equal terms to all groups in the community regardless of the beliefs and affiliations of their members, provided that the meetings be open to the public.

16 Organizing the Clock

It takes a long, long time to become a physician: four years of medical school after four years of college, then two or three years of internship, and often, finally, two or three years as a resident doctor in a hospital. By then the physicians are ready to begin their careers. But even then the work of preparation is not finished. They still have to devote much time to perfecting their skills. They have to live their professions twenty-four hours a day. If and when they become successful, it is in large measure because they have been willing to devote time, that most precious of all commodities, to work.

Your work in reading, though not in a class with medical training, is like it at least insofar as it demands a willingness on your part to devote time to it. "But," you say, "I have too much to do already." What you probably mean is not that you have too much to do, but rather that you have too little time in which to do it. Here, then, are two suggestions for finding more time to read: Organize yourself, and improve your reading habits.

Do you know some successful people? Is there a one of them who is not well organized? Probably not. Successful people in business, government, or almost any field you can mention organize themselves efficiently and budget their time. They realize the value of time very acutely, and they value it as a miser does his money. Ask the most successful people you know which they think is more important to them in their present status, time or money. They will probably say time. One of Benjamin Franklin's maxims said, "Dost thou love life? Then do not squander time, for that is the stuff life is made of." Not that you shouldn't use a reasonable amount for rest and relaxation, but most of us squander time in front of the tube or daydreaming about what we will do with our first million dollars.

Allot part of your time to serious reading, and deal with your first million when you get it. If you feel that reading is really important to you, you must find or take the time you need for doing it.

There is no best time for reading. It is true that there are certain periods during the day when your energy is at a low ebb. For most of us one of these periods comes an hour or two before the evening meal. However, the periods vary with individuals. The best time for you depends on the organization of your day. It is therefore important to know what that time is and to use it for your reading work.

Many people insist that they already know how their day is organized, and they say they are aware of their "most alert" periods, yet they simply cannot find enough time for reading. The Application Exercise for this chapter suggests that you make a record of your daily activities to find out just how your time is spent. Keeping a record is a simple matter if you are willing to be systematic and if you are curious about what happens to your time. After a week of keeping tabs you will know how you spend your time and can change your schedule if the facts warrant a change.

Now a word about improving your reading habits to find more time. If you read relatively simple fiction, like Pearl Buck's *The Good Earth*, at the average adult reading rate of approximately 250 to 300 words per minute, you now realize that you could read it quite as well, if not better, at twice that rate—with the right kind of effort. One high-school student who worked hard to improve reading habits read *The Good Earth* at 600 words per minute, with excellent comprehension. People have read over 900 words per minute with the same excellent comprehension. True, they had become very skillful readers; but they were not superhuman. Also, they did not skip any of the material but read every line. Think of the amount of material they could cover while someone else was meandering along at, say, 300 words per minute. Three times as much. Is it not obvious why time is not the problem for such a person that it may be for you?

These rapid readers did not develop their efficient reading skills overnight. They devoted time to the job and worked seriously at it. Happily, unlike the amount of time necessary to become a physician, the time to become a skillful reader can be counted in weeks. Many people have doubled their reading rates in four weeks without sacrifice of comprehension. For others it may take a little longer. But if you can double your reading rate in a month or two, is it not worthwhile in terms of both time and pleasure? To achieve this end, you should be willing to devote some time each day to your reading program. Set aside the time and devote it exclusively to improving your reading. Allow no days off. If you do take a vacation from reading after the first week or two, you hazard the chance of slipping back where you started.

When you finish this chapter you will have completed the first part of this book, which covers most of the important reading skills. You should by then have formed a solid foundation on which to begin a lifetime of skillful reading. If you have the will, you will find the time to read. This is the same will that you must exercise in replacing your old inefficient reading habits with new ones. Time and will power are what you need.

Work hard at your assigned task and practice your improved habits whenever you pick up a book, leaf through a magazine, or read the newspaper. You must keep practicing.

Average rate for Chapter 16: 475 wpm. Turn to the Comprehension Check on page 125.

Application Exercise: Chapter 16

Sticking to a Schedule

Almost every time you turn a page in this book you are asked to time yourself, but this time you are asked to make a different kind of timing operation. First, though, read the paragraphs below.

When Benjamin Franklin was about twenty-five, he devised a plan for "arriving at moral perfection." As part of his plan he drew up a list of virtues, and among these was Order, about which he said: "Let all your things have their places; let each part of your business have its time." In his *Autobiography* Franklin explains how he made a daily chart of his activities so he could organize himself more effectively. He found, however, that once he had established an orderly schedule, it was not easy to stick to it. He commented on this difficulty as follows:

Franklin the Incorrigible

"My scheme of ORDER gave me the most trouble; and I found that tho' it might be practicable where a man's business was such as to leave him the <u>disposition</u> of his time . . . it was not possible to be exactly observed by a master, who must mix with the world, and often receive people of business at their own hours. *Order*, too, with regard to places for things, papers, etc., I found extremely difficult to acquire. I had not been early accustomed to it, and, having an exceeding good memory, I was not so sensible of the inconvenience attending want of method. This article, therefore, cost me so much painful attention, and my faults in it <u>vexed</u> me so much, and I made so little progress in amendment, and had such frequent relapses, that I was almost ready to give up the attempt, and content myself with a faulty character in that respect, like the man who, in buying an ax of a smith, my neighbour, desired to have the whole of its surface as bright as the edge. The smith consented to grind it bright for him if he would turn the wheel; he turn'd, while the smith press'd the broad face of the ax hard and heavily on the stone, which made the turning of it very fatiguing. The man came every now and then from the wheel to see how the work went on, and at length would take his ax as it was, without farther grinding. 'No,' said the smith, 'turn on, turn on; we shall have it bright by-and-by; as yet, it is only speckled.' 'Yes,' says the man, *'but I think I like a speckled ax best.'* And I believe this may have been the case with many, who, having, for want of some such means as I employ'd, found the difficulty of obtaining good and breaking bad habits in other points of vice and virtue, have given up the

71

struggle, and concluded that '*a speckled ax was best*'; for something, that pretended to be reason, was every now and then suggesting to me that such extreme nicety as I exacted of myself might be a kind of <u>foppery</u> in morals, which, if it were known, would make me ridiculous; that a perfect character might be attended with the inconvenience of being envied and hated; and that a benevolent man should allow a few faults in himself, to keep his friends <u>in countenance</u>.

"In truth, I found myself <u>incorrigible</u> with respect to Order; and now I am grown old, and my memory bad, I feel very sensibly the want of it. But, on the whole, tho' I never arrived at the perfection I had been so ambitious of obtaining, but fell far short of it, yet I was, by the endeavour, a better and a happier man than I otherwise should have been if I had not attempted it."

Now check the chart of daily activities you made for your weekly schedule when you worked on the Application Exercise for Chapter 2. Revise it in light of your experience to date.

1. Is it sufficiently flexible?
2. Do you review material *before* class?
3. Are you able to carry out a plan for recreational reading?
4. Are your free hours really free of study?
5. What revisions are possible in the light of new understanding about "hard" and "easy" reading?
6. In the light of your revised estimates, is it possible to find time for a creative outlet such as recreational painting, singing, or writing?
7. If you are having difficulty sticking to your schedule, as did Benjamin Franklin, what do you believe is the chief cause of the difficulty? Is it the imperfection of the schedule? Were you too optimistic? Were you too ambitious?

17 Developing Curiosity

The previous chapters have emphasized some of the basic skills that should help you master fundamental reading tasks more effectively. But what of reading of the less immediately useful kind, the kind James Russell Lowell had in mind when he spoke of reading that "admits us to the whole world of thought and fancy and imagination"? This question is too often left unanswered in our colleges. Yet it is this kind of reading that leaves the strongest mark on us. Lowell also said, "Few men learn the highest use of books. After lifelong study many a man discovers too late that to have had the philosopher's stone availed nothing without the philosopher to use it."

Some years ago, when the author faced his first class of students in an introduction to literature course, he tried to impress them with the values of "nonutilitarian" reading, that is, the reading we do other than to get a good mark in class or to learn a fact that will prove useful. When he discussed what Bacon wrote about studies serving to delight and added that man does not live by bread alone, the blank look on the students' faces made him wonder if he should have chosen to be a bricklayer rather than a teacher of literature.

If the author were to face that class again, these are the reasons he would give for "nonutilitarian" reading. First of all, we should read to experience. Perhaps we can't take a trip to Europe, but we can share this experience with an author who has. Not only does a book take us to countries we can't visit ourselves, it can take us into the most fascinating place in the world, a person's mind. Good biographies of famous painters or writers try to reveal, often through letters or personal journals, what was going through their subjects' minds while they produced their masterpieces. Although works that offer the fullness of experience of another life often take years to produce, when they make contact with our minds, the impact has a chance of being permanent. We can't experience what these people have, but we can share their feelings through reading.

We read to satisfy our curiosity about these and many other things. In all of history most of the great discoveries have been made by men and women who were driven not by the desire to be useful but merely by the desire to satisfy their curiosity. A noted scientist, Abraham Flexner, who was for many years director of the famous Institute for Advanced Studies at Princeton, claims that curiosity brought about most of the important scientific contributions. "Curiosity," he says, "which may or may not eventuate in something useful, is probably the outstanding characteristic of modern thinking. It is not new. It goes back to Galileo,

Bacon, and to Sir Isaac Newton, and it must be absolutely unhampered. Institutions of learning should be devoted to the cultivation of curiosity and the less they are deflected by considerations of immediacy of application, the more likely they are to contribute not only to human welfare but to the equally important satisfaction of intellectual interest which may indeed be said to have become the ruling passion of intellectual life in modern times."

We should read, therefore, both to satisfy and develop our curiosity. Why, for example, do people act the way they do? What controls them? A psychology or sociology text will lend some insight into this problem, but more fascinating, perhaps, are Edith Wharton's *Ethan Frome* or Kate Chopin's *Awakening*. Are you curious about the peculiarity of certain personality types? Flannery O'Connor and Eudora Welty look closely at this subject in their stories. Strength of character? Read Willa Cather's *My Antonia*. Psychological penetration? Read Katherine Anne Porter's stories in *Flowering Judas*. Do you understand how tenant farmers feel when corporations take over their farms? Read John Steinbeck's *The Grapes of Wrath*. Books like these, which may seem "nonutilitarian," both develop and satisfy our curiosity. As Flexner says, don't be "deflected by considerations of immediacy of application."

Read to get out of a mental rut. Read, in other words, for some of the same reasons you go to the movies. You want a change from your regular routine. You want to forget your troubles. You want to become someone else by identifying yourself with this or that hero or heroine and by losing yourself in a story. In short, read "nonutilitarian" books for relief from the humdrum routine of life.

Another reason for such reading is to help ourselves face the future more intelligently. A student may see no "use" in reading George Orwell's *1984* or Aldous Huxley's *Brave New World*, for example, but both these books present striking pictures of what a regimented world would be like. Is this useful reading? The answer is yes, in proportion to your interest in the future. Of what use was it to Thomas Jefferson, a plantation owner, to read John Locke's *Essay on Civil Government*? By rights he should have been reading the colonial equivalent of farm bulletins and labor-management pamphlets. Fortunately for America, his "nonutilitarian" reading proved very useful in framing the Declaration of Independence and the Bill of Rights.

Read for appreciation and understanding. The more you know about the game of baseball, the more you appreciate it. As you learn about catcher's signals, pick-off plays, the hit-and-run, and sacrifices, the game becomes more interesting. After you have watched a few major league games, you appreciate the skill of the players. Just so with reading. The more you read about the life of Lincoln, the more you appreciate what he gave American life. Familiarity with the details of human experience, whether about baseball, Lincoln's life, or Samoan marriage customs, increases our ability to understand and appreciate that experience.

These, then, are some reasons for "nonutilitarian" reading. The following chapters will help you to deal more effectively with this kind of reading.

Record your rate here: _____

Average rate for Chapter 17: 490 wpm. Turn to the Comprehension Check on page 126.

Application Exercise: Chapter 17

Reading Your Palm

1. What is your inner nature? You could check your horoscope, or read Tarot cards, or go to a fortune teller. More rationally, you could look inside your mind. How do you behave in making choices? Why do you make the choices you do?

Listed next are categories of books. Indicate those you like by checking the appropriate categories:

_____ adventure (action)

_____ detective (clever? hard-boiled?)

_____ horror (terror? fright?)

_____ occult (the inexplicable)

_____ religious

_____ historical (local? authentic?)

_____ romance (young love? historical?)

_____ romance (overcomes odds?)

_____ topical (urban? suburban?)

_____ school (early days? current?)

_____ sea stories

_____ army stories (navy? marines? air force?)

_____ animal stories

_____ science fiction (the future?)

_____ biographies (living? historical?)

_____ art history (drama? music? other arts?)

_____ famous authors (name the author)

_____ poetry (traditional? contemporary?)

_____ drama (traditional? contemporary?)

_____ photography (other hobbies?)

2. What do the categories mean to you? The answer probably lies in your reasons for reading. You may say, for example, "I like action, adventure . . . " Or you may say, "I like well-developed characters, people I would recognize on the street." In other words, your answer may uncover more than the surface, and it may well lead to self-discovery. Look into your consciousness and answer for each category you checked.

3. How does knowledge of your reading categories lead to self-discovery?

Do books help you live vicariously?

Do you read to satisfy your curiosity about how things work?

Do you read to see why people act the way they do?

Do you read to find the beauty, grace, and power in the world of artistic endeavor?

Do you read to escape from pressures that build up?

Does your pattern of reading reveal the kind of person you are? Such self-discovery helps us see ourselves more clearly and often with renewed insight into our own behavior.

Richard Wright, before his death in 1960 often considered a leading black writer, confesses that his life was changed by reading. In *Black Boy* he tells of seeing an editorial saying that H. L. Mencken was a fool. This made him want to read Mencken's books, which he did, by borrowing a white man's library card. Then he turned to other books, Sinclair Lewis's *Main Street* and *Babbitt*. He says, "Reading grew into a passion . . . [it] was like a drug, a dope . . . the novels created moods in which I lived for days." Have you ever lived in "created moods"?

18 *Evaluating a Book*

In order to be a skillful reader you need more than the right habits of moving your eyes across the page. You need to be able to think actively and creatively. This seems very obvious. Somewhat less obvious is the fact that the thinking we do while we read is concerned not merely with understanding but also with evaluating.

All readers worth their salt are critics, whether they know it or not. They evaluate literature in the light of certain standards of taste that they set up or that are established by custom. How do professional critics evaluate books? And who are they?

Competent critics are people like Matthew Arnold, John Ruskin, and in our time, and generally speaking, the people who write reviews for such national weeklies as *The New York Times Book Review* or *The New Yorker*, or such "little" magazines as *The Virginia Quarterly Review, The Paris Review,* or the *Antioch Review.*

How do critics evaluate? Except in unusual instances, magazines of limited circulation seldom review a book that the unpaid reviewer doesn't like. They tell what's good about a book, how it is like or unlike other books, and how strongly it is recommended. Often the reviewers are experts in the field and their opinion is eagerly sought.

The larger-circulation periodicals also ask experts in the field to review books, and novels are usually reviewed by experienced novelists, who try to tell readers how the novel compares with other novels of its kind, how well the author has handled the subject, and how well the novel is crafted (characterization, plot, setting, etc.). In other words, they go into detail about why they liked it. They don't use formulas, and their measuring scale is based on a cultivated taste. They are aware of various principles of criticism, such as those of Aristotle and Edgar Allan Poe, but you seldom catch them in the act of mentioning those principles. Also they take pride in forming an independent opinion. They are unlikely to say, "It's a simple plot I can relate to because it keeps moving and has a happy ending."

Sometimes they enjoy panning a work, as when a reviewer said of Ibsen's great play, *A Doll's House,* that it was as though someone had dramatized the cooking of a Sunday dinner, or as when Twain said of the famous German composer, Richard Wagner, that his music was better than it sounds.

Critics are human and are in general respectable representatives of the human race. They are people who read widely, have a broad cultural background, and have opinions we value because they have been there.

How can you become a critical reader? Well, as we just finished saying, you need to establish a reasonably broad cultural background by reading widely. You need to be there. Yet, if in your own past experience you can find an instance in your life that fits the author's theme, you have already begun the process of critical reading. You have already begun to be there. Willa Cather's delightful story "Neighbor Rosicky" will serve as an example. It is the story of Anton Rosicky in the last few months of his life, his failing heart about to give out, striving to bring his son's wife, Polly, into the Bohemian family in rural Nebraska, Cather's native territory. Anyone who has been drawn into the family of another can sympathize with both Anton's and Polly's situation. It is a story of family, the influence of environment on the characters, and the theme Cather was the preeminent practitioner of, the gift of sympathy. When the readers recognize the gift, they have entered Cather's realm and are reading critically. "Critically" here means sympathetically. They are bringing their own backgrounds to bear on the story and its implications.

Or if, on the basis of their experience, readers take exception to an author's point of view, they are reading critically. If they are reading a persuasive article and recognize the emotional basis of the writer's appeal, they are critical readers. To some extent you do this now.

As a critical reader you will begin to feel that the printed page is not sacred. Authors make mistakes, they exaggerate, and they overgeneralize just like the rest of us. Not to recognize this fact and to swallow all they have to say without even attempting to chew on it is to invite a bad case of indigestion. Too many say, "It must be so; the book says so."

Be critical of yourself as well as of writers. Perhaps they are right and you are wrong. Reexamine what they say. Perhaps they didn't say what you thought they said. Are you sure you know what they mean? In a particularly difficult passage it may pay to test each phrase, or even each key word, independently. Examine them in every possible light; then make your final evaluation of them as they stand in the context.

Good readers are not only critics, they are also creators. Their tools of creation are the same as the author's—their imaginations. Using imagination, good readers recreate the author's thought. Consider Shakespeare's *Hamlet*, for example. An active, imaginative, and creative reading of the play would bring readers a feeling of deep satisfaction, because they will begin to share in Shakespeare's imagination when they grasp the play through their own. The actress who portrays Ophelia on the stage must go even further. When her whole mind is pervaded by the imagination of Shakespeare, her response to the playwright's lines will be creative indeed. She reads and reads until, steeped in the verses, she finds the word groupings coming as naturally as if they were her own.

Creative and critical reading is the supreme test of skillful readers. These skills require every other reading skill plus plenty of intellect, and they demand that readers use the store of experience they have gained both from everyday life and from the printed page. Above all, they require an inquiring mind and an ability to respond creatively.

Record your rate here: _____
Average rate for Chapter 18: 500 wpm. Turn to the Comprehension
Check on page 127.

Application Exercise: Chapter 18

Speaking Critically

Aristotle's Critical Limits

Do Aristotle's ideas seem out of date? *The Poetics* was written in the
fourth century B.C., but many critics feel the principles have not been
improved upon. In the exercises that follow you will be asked to determine their timeliness.

Aristotle explains that the object of art is to show people in action.
He says that for dramatic action (theater or film) to reveal the fullness
and futility of life (as opposed to comic situations), it depends on certain
limits. The five limits follow.

1. The action takes place within a single revolution of the sun.
    Question: Why does a twenty-four-hour period for the action of a modern
    drama (play or film) make sense? When doesn't it make sense? (Assume for
    the moment that what we speak of as flashbacks were an accepted principle
    in Aristotle's day.)
2. The emotions of pity and fear, excited by the plot, are purged or released.
    Question: What does it mean to be purged of pity and fear? Name a horror
    movie that makes its appeal on this basis. Do you emerge drained? Would
    you argue against Aristotle and say that other emotions (love, hate, etc.)
    ought to be involved? Cite a modern film to support your answer.
3. Situations in the plot are reversed or the unknown is recognized.
    Question: Cite a modern drama where the situations of the plot are
    reversed or the unknown is recognized. Must drama have these charac-
    teristics today? Specify a reversal and indicate why it is necessary.
4. The hero falls from high estate to low through a flaw in his character
    (usually pride).
    Question: Willy Loman in Arthur Miller's *Death of a Salesman* is often cited
    as a hero (he's no king but he's heroic because he represents all modern
    humanity) who falls from high estate (he was once happy and on top of the
    world when his boys were growing up) to low (he finally commits suicide)
    through a flaw in his character (he couldn't be honest with himself and was
    too proud of his make-believe world). Cite heros or heroines in modern
    drama who fall from high estate to low through a flaw in character. If a
    drama does not come to mind, consider *Children of a Lesser God*.
5. The unraveling of the plot comes through the action of the plot itself, not by
    some artificial device (God from the machine).
    Question: Cite a modern drama where some artificial device solves the
    problem of the plot. "The Seventh Cavalry to the Rescue" is one such
    artificial solution. Name another (perhaps from science fiction) and tell why
    it is artificial. Then tell why an artificial solution is unsatisfactory.

79

Nonprofessional Critics

What do ordinary people (as opposed to professional critics) like about plot and characters? When a group of storytellers sat around and commented on each other's stories, they responded in a bewildering variety of ways—bewildering because the reasons were often contradictory.

Here are some of their responses about why a plot is appealing:

"It's a simple plot I can relate to because it keeps moving and has a happy ending."

"The plot is about a subject that fascinates me." (love, sex, the West, the South, violent action, the occult, science fiction, animals, humor)

"The plot is intense, does not have a pat formula, keeps you guessing, and has a snap ending or unusual twist."

And why do characters appeal?

"Characters must be believable, strong, and ingenious."

"I need to relate to the characters, to be able to picture them, to know them through their actions, to learn about life through them."

While the responses may not be couched in the language of Aristotle, they say in ordinary words what people today think. Should fiction illuminate life? ("I want to learn about life through characters.")

Omitted in the responses of many people were answers to certain questions. Try your hand at answering some of them.

1. Should fiction reveal insight into truth? (What kind of truth?)
2. Should the quality of the author's style be considered? Why? What makes a good style?
3. Must there be a change in the main character over the course of the piece of fiction? Why? What's the difference between an anecdote and a story?
4. Should the reader sense a writer's deep engagement with the subject—so deep that the reader begins to feel an intimate sharing? If so, why?
5. Should there be room for new techniques such as minimalism, theater of the absurd, or metafiction (fiction about the nature of fiction itself)? What if you don't like the new techniques?
6. How necessary is a ring of authenticity to the story?

19 *Digging Deeper*

Many people object to analyzing a poem or a story. They feel that, somehow or other, a dissection will destroy its beauty or its mood. They don't like to take a thing apart for fear it might never become a "living" whole again. Even if one explains that the instrument of dissection is their own mind and that a piece of literature will become much more alive and meaningful when they learn to see the relation of its parts to the whole, they still react violently against the idea.

But there is no other way to find the essential qualities of a good work of art than by examining it, so to speak, with X-ray eyes. Before the X-ray was invented, physicians had to guess about the arrangement of the parts of a living organism. They had to rely on an imperfect method. But when they could examine with the X-ray, the preciseness of their knowledge increased enormously. And note this: Their subject remained alive while they were investigating. They did not worry about destroying the beauty of the organism, just as the patients did not complain about having their inner selves invaded. The X-ray was universally acclaimed as a useful tool to greater knowledge and understanding, and there was less need for intuitive medical analysis.

Just so can logical analysis help the reader of a book. Emily Dickinson can say that she knows good poetry intuitively because, "I feel physically as if the top of my head were taken off"; but to understand and appreciate a book, readers should attempt to discover what its parts are, how they relate to each other, and what binds them into one unified whole. As we have already said, they do not endanger the living character of a book. Rather, a careful analysis of a book is the best way to bring it to life, to make it become vital and beautiful. Alexander Pope once said that when you dissect an insect in order to determine what makes it live, you lose life at the moment you detect it. But, as Pope would be the first to remind us, a book is not an insect. The moment you detect what makes a book live, it becomes forever even more alive. And you detect what makes it live by dissecting it.

A very poor book may be compared to an amoeba, the simplest form of animal life. It has little structure, being merely a mass of relatively unrelated parts flowing unpredictably and without pattern. A very good book, on the other hand, may be compared to *homo sapiens*, the most complex form of animal life. It has a very complete and thoroughly unified structure; the parts are closely related and move in definite and determinable ways toward a goal.

You job as a reader of a good book is to determine its structure, the relationship of its parts, and the way it moves toward its goal. You go about determining these things by asking an imaginary question of authors. You ask what the book is about, that is, what is its main point. In back of this question is your thinking about the book's unity. You are looking for the theme about which the book moves. Once you think you have determined the main point, try stating it in as few words as possible. Even in such an immense novel as *Gone With the Wind* the theme can be stated in a few simple and familiar words: Girl meets boy; girl gets boy; girl loses boy. You cannot always reduce a book to such simple terms, but when you do thus strip it to its barest essentials, you begin to find out what makes it live. In *Gone With the Wind*, for example, you find that the essence of part one is: girl meets boy; part two: girl gets boy; and part three: girl loses boy. The Civil War acts as an effective backdrop for this ancient story formula.

Next you should be able to indicate what the parts of the book are, as we have shown, in very general terms, for *Gone With the Wind*. On a simple level it works like this. When you go to a play you may notice that each act is, in a sense, a play in itself. Consider Arthur Miller's two-act play, *Death of a Salesman*, for example. In Act One, Willy Loman's life is revealed to the audience. His dreams and ambitions have been devoted to a false criterion of success—namely, to be well liked and to make money at the expense of everything else. Willy tells his sons, "The man who makes an appearance in the business world, the man who creates personal interest, is the man who gets ahead. Be liked and you will never want." At the end of the act the audience senses quite deeply the tragedy of Willy's existence. The act is a complete unit, for it shows Willy's fall from high estate to low, and it leaves unresolved only the means of his final descent to death. Act Two heightens the tragedy when the sons revert hopelessly to the same false standards that led to Willy's failure. This act is a complete unit also, and with a few changes it might stand alone as a well-integrated play. Alone, each act would present a fascinating study; together they form a deeply moving tragedy, each act contributing its share to our understanding of a man who destroys himself.

The principle of analyzing parts is the same for a novel or a poem. In a novel you consider the chapters; in a poem, the stanzas or cantos. These divisions make up the apparent structure of a work as the author saw it. You may see it another way, but the important thing is this: The good reader sees the whole, the parts, and the relationship of the parts— to dig deeper is to analyze the author's style and ultimately the individual words.

Average rate for Chapter 19: over 500 wpm. Turn to the Comprehension Check on page 128.

Application Exercise: Chapter 19

Analyzing a Sample

Read the short analysis of Lincoln's Gettysburg Address, which shows how some of the principles of analyzing may be applied. When you have finished, analyze the Declaration of Independence.

The Gettysburg Address

Fourscore and seven years ago our fathers brought forth on this continent a new nation, conceived in liberty, and dedicated to the proposition that all men are created equal.

Now we are engaged in a great civil war, testing whether that nation, or any nation so conceived and so dedicated, can long endure. We are met on a great battlefield of that war. We have come to dedicate a portion of that field as a final resting place for those who here gave their lives that that nation might live. It is altogether fitting and proper that we should do this.

But, in a larger sense, we cannot dedicate—we cannot <u>consecrate</u>—we cannot hallow—this ground. The brave men, living and dead, who struggled here, have consecrated it far above our poor power to add or detract. The world will little note nor long remember what we say here, but it can never forget what they did here. It is for us, the living, rather, to be dedicated here to the unfinished work which they who fought here have thus far so nobly advanced. It is rather for us to be here dedicated to the great task remaining before us— that from these honored dead we take increased devotion to that cause for which they gave their last full measure of devotion; that we here highly resolve that these dead shall not have died in vain; that this nation, under God, shall have a new birth of freedom; and that government of the people, by the people, for the people, shall not perish from the earth.

Analysis

Purpose

The beginning and end of the speech indicate that Lincoln was attempting to define the American democratic philosophy. The middle of the speech indicates that he was dedicating a cemetery. This much the speech itself tells us. The historical background of the speech reveals that Lincoln, who had been accused of making jokes about the dead a year before, wanted the people to know his true character. Thus, the emphasis on dignity and sincerity. It also reveals that pressure was put on Lincoln to speak out for democracy, popular government, and the masses.

Language

Figurative language links the time order of Lincoln's speech to the basic cycle of life: "our fathers brought forth a new nation, conceived in liberty" (birth); "and dedicated" (baptism); "long endure" (life); "final resting place" (death); and "new birth of freedom" (rebirth). The biblical tone of the speech ("Four score and seven," "our fathers," "dedicated," "consecrate," and "hallow") makes it appealing to those whose feelings stem from religious thought.

Organization

The logical, chronological, and spatial organization of the speech is as follows: logical—(1) these ceremonies are appropriate, but (2) the living cannot dedicate this ground; instead (3) the living should themselves be dedicated; chronological—from past to present to future; spatial—the subject is narrowed from continent to nation to battlefield, and then enlarged from this nation to, finally, the world.

Now analyze the following selection from The Declaration of Independence. First reduce it to five or six sentences and show how one part is related to another, then comment on the purpose and on the appropriateness of the language.

The Declaration of Independence

When, in the course of human events, it becomes necessary for one people to dissolve the political bands which have connected them with another, and to assume among the powers of the earth, the separate and equal station to which the Laws of Nature and of Nature's God entitle them, a decent respect to the opinions of mankind requires that they should declare the causes which impel them to the separation.

We hold these truths to be self-evident, that all men are created equal, that they are endowed by their Creator with certain <u>unalienable</u> rights, that among these are Life, Liberty and the pursuit of Happiness. That to secure these rights, governments are instituted among men, deriving their just powers from the consent of the governed. That whenever any form of government becomes destructive of these ends, it is the right of the people to alter or to abolish it, and to institute new government, laying its foundation on such principles and organizing its powers in such form, as to them shall seem most likely to effect their safety and happiness. <u>Prudence</u>, indeed, will dictate that governments long established should not be changed for light and transient causes; and accordingly all experience hath shewn, that mankind are more disposed to suffer, while evils are sufferable, than to right themselves by abolishing the forms to which they are accustomed. But when a long train of abuses and <u>usurpations</u>, pursuing invariably the same object, evidence a design to reduce them under absolute <u>despotism</u>, it is their right, it is their duty, to throw off such government, and to provide new guards for their future security. Such has been the patient sufferance of these colonies; and such is now the necessity which constrains them to alter their former systems of government. The history of the present king of Great Britain is a history of repeated injuries and usurpations, all having in direct object the establishment of an absolute tyranny over these states. To prove this, let facts be submitted to a candid world. . . .

20 *Setting Up Standards*

If you are enthusiastic about sports, you recognize immediately a poor performance by an athlete or by a team. You know from having watched many sports events that a certain standard of performance is expected. You also know that when athletes—for example, tennis players—enter the professional ranks, they have to meet the highest standards. If they don't, they quickly find themselves ranked with the amateurs.

People who publish a novel have also entered the professional ranks, and they also must meet the highest standards. If they don't, they also quickly find themselves ranked with the amateurs.

We have all been in groups where athletics or novels are being discussed, and we know that in such groups there are always those who sound off merely for the sake of hearing their own voices. They glean some items of information or opinion from someone who, they think, is really "in the know." Then they spring this "knowledge" at the first opportunity. They work it into the conversation and hope that we will regard them as authorities. Most of the time, however, we are not fooled—at least not for long.

In contrast to false authorities are people who really know. Their remarks carry the weight of wide and long experience. In the case of athletics, such people have either been players themselves or have carefully observed a large number of sports events. They are credible authorities because they have had the opportunity to compare many performances. They know when an athletic performance is better than average, because they know what excellence is. The same is true of the people who know novels. Their opinion is respected either because they are novelists themselves or because they have read, intelligently, a great many novels. Their remarks carry conviction because they base them on experience and intimate acquaintance with the novelist's art. As they say at the race track, they "talk like a person with a tip straight from the horse's mouth."

What are some of the standards by which we measure a book? First of all, there is the matter of legibility. Perhaps this seems almost too obvious, but it certainly does influence our judgment. To judge a book you must be able to read it easily. The size of type, color of page and print, and size of margins should not be a hindrance to reading. Next, there is a matter of language, a standard that can vary from the simple to the extremely complex. For most of us, the book must be written in a language we can read, not Sanskrit or Egyptian or Zulu, but English. However, we know all too well that a book can be written in English and still not be easily understood. Our judgment for such a book becomes one of style; we consider the author's manner of expression. In reading to gain knowledge, it is sufficient if the author imparts information clearly. When we read a book as a work of art, we look for clarity of expression, but for something more, too. It is at this point of "something more" that a consideration of standards progresses from the merely useful to the aesthetic—to the consideration of artistic beauty.

What is the "something more" we search for in the writing of a novel or short story? One thing we are especially conscious of is the language used. Not only must it be on a mature level (most adults resent having to read a version of *Tom Sawyer* adapted for fourth-grade use), but it must be appropriate to the design of the story. The matter was admirably stated by Edgar Allan Poe, who said, "In the whole composition, there should be no word written, of which the tendency, direct or indirect, is not to the one pre-established design." But employing the standard of language that Poe sets up means determining the author's purpose, what Poe calls "the one pre-established design." There is a style for sarcasm, for irony, for mystery, for horror, and so on.

Let one example from the last paragraph of Poe's "The Fall of the House of Usher" serve to show what he considered to be an appropriate style for horror. "From that chamber, and from that mansion, I fled aghast. The storm was still abroad in all its wrath as I found myself crossing the old causeway. Suddenly there shot along the path a wild light, and I turned to see whence a gleam so unusual could have issued; for the vast house and its shadows were alone behind me. The radiance was that of the full, setting and blood-red moon, which now shone vividly through that once barely-discernible fissure . . . in a zigzag direction to the base." There is an appropriate style for every purpose, and readers should judge the style in the light of whatever the purpose happens to be.

There are still other standards by which literature should be judged. Most of them are concerned with what we shall call, for want of a better phrase, enrichment of life. The critical reader must ask: "Does this book help me understand human nature a little better?" This question is one that will be accompanied by others: "Is this author's point of view about human nature a reasonable one? Is it possible that, given these characters and this plot, people would act like this? Is the plot plausible? Are the characters true to life?" The questions, of course, will depend on the work at hand, but they all lead to our asking: "Do these authors really have anything to say to me, and shall I change or enlarge my view of life because of what they say?"

We all set up standards of our own by which we judge other people's views of life. No one else can decide your standards. To some degree, therefore, a work of literature is good or bad or somewhere in between good and bad, as you see it.

Record your rate here: _____

Average rate on Chapter 20: over 500 wpm. Turn to the Comprehension Check on page 129.

Application Exercise: Chapter 20

From Mark Twain's "Fenimore Cooper's Literary Offenses" (1895)

Twain's devastation of James Fenimore Cooper, written fifty-four years after *The Deerslayer*, is of course a masterpiece of satire, and readers are advised to note the enthusiasm and relish with which Twain peppered his "judgments." He meant to be funny, and most people feel he succeeded. But was Twain being fair in his exaggeration? To answer, readers need to know what is exaggeration and what isn't.

Here are two points of exaggeration. Find at least three others and underline and explain them.

1. "Cooper has scored 114 offenses against literary art out of a possible 115." Twain is here making a humorous analogy to target shooting. He assumes the reader will understand that he has invented the idea of 115 literary offenses.
2. "There are nineteen rules governing literary art in the domain of romantic fiction—some say twenty-two." Twain is pretending there are a certain number of rules and that the rules of romantic fiction can be enumerated as if the rules were part of a scientific study. He reinforces the pretense by indicating that experts disagree as to the number.

From Mark Twain's essay (1895)
Fenimore Cooper's Literary Offenses

The Pathfinder and *The Deerslayer* stand at the head of Cooper's novels as artistic creations. There are others of his works which contain parts as perfect as are to be found in these, and scenes even more thrilling. Not one can be compared with either of them as a finished whole.

The defects in both of these tales are comparatively slight. They were pure works of art.—*Prof. Lounsbury.*

The five tales reveal an extraordinary fullness of invention. . . . One of the very greatest characters in fiction, Natty Bumppo. . . .

The craft of the woodsman, the tricks of the trapper, all the delicate art of the forest, were familiar to Cooper from his youth up.—*Prof. Brander Matthews.*

Cooper is the greatest artist in the domain of romantic fiction yet produced by America.—*Wilkie Collins.*

It seems to me that it was far from right for the Professor of English Literature in Yale, the Professor of English Literature in Columbia, and Wilkie Collins to deliver opinions of Cooper's literature without having read some of it. It would have been much more <u>decorous</u> to keep silent and let persons talk who have read Cooper.

Cooper's art has some defects. In one place in *Deerslayer*, and in the restricted space of two-thirds of a page, Cooper has scored 114 offenses against literary art out of a possible 115. It breaks the record.

There are nineteen rules governing literary art in the domain of romantic fiction—some say twenty-two. In *Deerslayer* Cooper violated eighteen of them. These eighteen require:

1. That a tale shall accomplish something and arrive somewhere. But the *Deerslayer* tale accomplishes nothing and arrives in the air.

2. They require that the episodes of a tale shall be necessary parts of the tale, and shall help to develop it. But as the *Deerslayer* tale is not a tale, and accomplishes nothing and arrives nowhere, the episodes have no rightful place in the work, since there was nothing for them to develop.

3. They require that the <u>personages</u> in a tale shall be alive, except in the case of corpses, and that always the reader shall be able to tell the corpses from the others. But this detail has often been overlooked in the *Deerslayer* tale.

4. They require that the personages in a tale, both dead and alive, shall exhibit a sufficient excuse for being there. But this detail also has been overlooked in the *Deerslayer* tale.

5. They require that when the personages of a tale deal in conversation, the talk shall sound like human talk, and be talk such as human beings would be likely to talk in the given circumstances, and have a discoverable meaning, also a discoverable purpose, and a show of <u>relevancy</u>, and remain in the neighborhood of the subject in hand, and be interesting to the reader, and help out the tale, and stop when the people cannot think of anything more to say. But this requirement has been ignored from the beginning of the *Deerslayer* tale to the end of it.

6. They require that when the author describes the character of a personage in his tale, the conduct and conversation of that personage shall justify said description. But this law gets little to no attention in the *Deerslayer* tale, as Natty Bumppo's case will amply prove.

7. They require that when a personage talks like an illustrated, gilt-edged, tree-calf, hand-tooled, seven-dollar Friendship's Offering in the beginning of a paragraph, he shall not talk like a negro minstrel in the end of it. But this rule is flung down and danced upon in the *Deerslayer* tale.

8. They require that <u>crass</u> stupidities shall not be played upon the reader as "the craft of the woodsman, the delicate art of the forest," by either the author or the people in the tale. But this rule is <u>persistently</u> violated in the *Deerslayer* tale.

9. They require that the personages of a tale shall confine themselves to possibilities and let miracles alone; or, if they venture a miracle,

the author must so plausibly set it forth as to make it look possible and reasonable. But these rules are not respected in the *Deerslayer* tale.

10. They require that the author shall make the reader feel a deep interest in the personages of his tale and in their fate; and that he shall make the reader love the good people in the tale and hate the bad ones. But the reader of the *Deerslayer* tale dislikes the good people in it, is indifferent to the others, and wishes they would all get drowned together.

11. They require that the characters in a tale shall be so clearly defined that the reader can tell beforehand what each will do in a given emergency. But in the *Deerslayer* tale this rule is vacated.

In addition to these large rules there are some little ones. These require that the author shall

12. *Say* what he is proposing to say, not merely come near it.

13. Use the right word, not its second cousin.

14. Eschew surplusage.

15. Not omit necessary details.

16. Avoid slovenliness of form.

17. Use good grammar.

18. Employ a simple and straightforward style.

Even these seven are coldly and persistently violated in the *Deerslayer* tale.

Cooper's gift in the way of invention was not a rich endowment; but such as it was he liked to work it, he was pleased with the effects, and indeed he did some quite sweet things with it. In his little box of stage-properties he kept six or eight cunning devices, tricks, artifices for his savages and woodsmen to deceive and circumvent each other with, and he was never so happy as when he was working these innocent things and seeing them go. A favorite one was to make a moccasined person tread in the tracks of the moccasined enemy, and thus hide his own trail. Cooper wore out barrels and barrels of moccasins in working that trick. Another stage-property that he pulled out of his box pretty frequently was his broken twig. He prized his broken twig above all the rest of his effects, and worked it the hardest. It is a restful chapter in any book of his when somebody doesn't step on a dry twig and alarm all the reds and whites for two hundred yards around. Every time a Cooper person is in peril, and absolute silence is worth four dollars a minute, he is sure to step on a dry twig. There may be a hundred handier things to step on, but that wouldn't satisfy Cooper. Cooper requires him to turn out and find a dry twig; and if he can't do it, go and borrow one. In fact, the Leatherstocking Series ought to have been called the Broken Twig Series.

21 *Looking for Truth*

What makes a book great? Mark Twain is supposed to have said that great books were those everybody recommends and no one reads. All people have their own lists of great books, and it would be foolish to insist on uniformity of opinion, but it is not foolish to try to express our ideas of what makes a book great. Doing so helps sharpen critical perception and makes us read with a keener appreciation.

Great literature is generally an original communication, a contribution to some unsolved problem of human life. Generally, too, such works have a notable style derived from the care with which the authors have fashioned their writing. It goes without saying that competent reading of great books requires a real effort of attention. In order to get the most out of such a book you must give your best to it.

James Russell Lowell emphasizes this point when he says, "Among books, certainly, there is much variety of company, ranging from the best to the worst, from Plato to Zola, and the first lesson in reading well is that which teaches us to distinguish between literature and merely printed matter. The choice lies wholly with ourselves. Every book we read may be made a round in the ever-lengthening ladder by which we climb to knowledge and to that temperance and serenity of mind which, as it is the ripest fruit of Wisdom, is also the sweetest. But this can only be if we read such books as make us think, and read them in such a way as helps them to do so, that is, by endeavoring to judge them, and thus to make them an exercise rather than a relaxation of the mind."

In his *Sesame and Lilies*, John Ruskin also speaks eloquently on the subject. "The author," he remarks, "has something to say which he perceives to be true and useful, or helpfully beautiful. So far as he knows, no one has yet said it; so far as he knows, no one else can say it. He is bound to say it, clearly and melodiously if he may; clearly at all events. In the sum of his life he finds this to be the thing, or group of things, manifest to him;—this, the piece of true knowledge, or sight, which his share of sunshine and earth has permitted him to seize. He would fain set it down forever; engrave it on rock, if he could, saying, 'This is the best of me: for the rest, I ate and drank, and slept, loved, and hated, like another; my life was as the vapour, and is not; but this I saw and knew; This, if anything of mine, is worth your memory.' That is his 'writing'; it is, in his small human way, and with whatever degree of true inspiration is in him, his inscription, or scripture. That is a 'Book'."

As great literature is a record of the best that people have thought and said, it certainly deserves the right kind of reading. Here are a few suggestions about the reading of great literature. Read first for sheer enjoyment. Since the great literary classics are worth more than one perusal, read the first time as an adventurer exploring a new world. When you finish, set the book aside for a few days. Think about it occasionally. Let it form its impression on your mind. Then, after a week or so—or a month if need be, go back to it. This time read it more carefully. If it is a work of fiction, start looking for the fine points of characterization and plot. Read to see what makes the work great.

The idea that great literature depends a good deal on the reader as well as the writer has often been expressed. Emerson was thinking about the reader in his American Scholar Address over 150 years ago when he spoke about poets and poetry. He emphasized the fact that the reader must bring an active mind to reading. No wise person, he contended, would read and accept blindly. Reading great literature is an activity that requires constant alertness. He said, "Great and heroic men have existed, who had almost no other information than by the printed page. I would say that it needs a strong head to bear that diet. One must be an inventor to read well. There is creative reading as well as creative writing. When the mind is braced by labor and invention, the page of whatever book we read becomes luminous with manifold allusion. Every sentence is doubly significant, and the sense of our author is as broad as the world."

Not many works of American literature are written with a "sense as broad as the world," but there are some American novels that critics agree deserve to be read as classics. They are Nathaniel Hawthorne's *The Scarlet Letter*, Herman Melville's *Moby-Dick*, and Mark Twain's *Huckleberry Finn*. Each can be read and reread and read yet again. Edith Warton, Willa Cather, and Kate Chopin also deserve close reading. Every time you enter the magic realm of one of these books, you will find something new, something that you somehow missed before. They are a joy to read.

Emerson, speaking of the keen delight of great literature, said, "It is remarkable the pleasure we derive from the best books. They impress us with the conviction that one nature wrote and the same reads. There is some awe mixed with the joy of our surprise, when this poet, who lived in some past world, says that which lies close to my own soul, that which I also had well nigh thought and said."

Remember that the authors of the books we now consider great did not write them merely for scholars. For the most part they wrote with great clarity for everyone who could read. Great books, then, are yours; they were not meant to be the possession of an elite few.

Average rate for Chapter 21: over 500 wpm. Turn to the Comprehension Check on page 130.

Application Exercise: Chapter 21

From Ralph Waldo Emerson's "American Scholar Address" (1837)

After reading this selection, apply what you have learned to answer the questions that follow.

The theory of books is noble. The scholar of the first age received into him the world around; <u>brooded</u> thereon; gave it the new arrangement of his own mind, and uttered it again. It came into him life; it went out from him truth. It came to him short-lived actions; it went out from him <u>immortal</u> thoughts. It came to him business; it went from him poetry. It was dead fact; now, it is quick thought. It can stand, and it can go. It now endures, it now flies, it now inspires. Precisely in proportion to the depth of mind from which it issued, so high does it soar, so long does it sing.

Or, I might say, it depends on how far the process had gone, of <u>transmuting</u> life into truth. In proportion to the completeness of the distillation, so will the purity and <u>imperishableness</u> of the product be. But none is quite perfect. As no air-pump can by any means make a perfect vacuum, so neither can any artist entirely exclude the conventional, the local, the perishable from his book, or write a book of pure thought, that shall be as efficient, in all respects, to a remote posterity, as to contemporaries, or rather to the second age. Each age, it is found, must write its own books; or rather, each generation for the next succeeding. The books of an older period will not fit this.

Yet hence arises a grave mischief. The sacredness which attaches to the act of creation, the act of thought, is transferred to the record. The poet chanting was felt to be a divine man: henceforth the chant is divine also. The writer was a just and wise spirit: henceforward it is settled the book is perfect; as love of the hero corrupts into worship of his statue. Instantly the book becomes <u>noxious</u>: the guide is a tyrant. The sluggish and perverted mind of the multitude, slow to open to the <u>incursions</u> of Reason, having once so opened, having once received this book, stands upon it, and makes an outcry if it is <u>disparaged</u>. Colleges are built on it. Books are written on it by thinkers, not by Man Thinking; by men of talent, that is, who start wrong, who set out from accepted dogmas, not from their own sight of principles. Meek young men grow up in libraries, believing it their duty to accept the views which Cicero, which Locke, which Bacon, have given; forgetful that Cicero, Locke, and Bacon were only young men in libraries when they wrote these books.

Hence, instead of Man Thinking, we have the bookworm. Hence the book-learned class, who value books, as such; not as related to nature and the human constitution, but as making a sort of Third Estate with the world and the soul. Hence the restorers of readings, the emendators, the bibliomaniacs of all degrees.

Books are the best of things, well used; abused, among the worst. What is the right use? What is the one which all means go to effect? They are for nothing but to inspire. I had better never see a book than to be warped by its attraction clean out of my own orbit, and made a satellite instead of a system. The one thing in the world, of value, is the active soul.

1. Emerson says, "It came into him life; it went out from him truth." Name a book you have read that fits that description, and tell why it seems to you to be "truth."
2. "Each generation [must write its books] for the next succeeding." Name a book you feel will be especially suitable for the next generation. What qualities make it seem suitable?
3. We have all found books that seemed "divine" when we read them, only to change our minds a few years later. Name a book that fits that description for you. Indicate, if you can, why you have changed your mind about it.
4. What is a bibliomaniac?
5. If the "right use" of the book is to inspire, name a book that inspired you. What was the source of that inspiration for you?
6. Emerson's address was delivered over 150 years ago. Does it still seem to you to contain germs of truth? If so, what does that suggest to you about the tired and dusty volumes of the past?

22 *Rereading Favorites*

Rereading favorite authors may seem a surprising suggestion, but it is a sound way of touching greatness and discovering something about yourself.

As one who has professed American literature in college classrooms for more than four decades, I have had the responsibility, colored with keen delight, of living with the greatest American authors day in and day out. How do I know they are great? Because the nature of my profession requires that I reread a novel, story, essay, or poem every time I teach it, and if a work cannot stand the test of countless rereadings, out it goes and I never assign it again. That happened to Hemingway's *For Whom the Bell Tolls*, to all of Sinclair Lewis's works, to most of William Saroyan's, and Thomas Wolfe's.

But if, like Twain's *The Adventures of Huckleberry Finn* or Thoreau's *Walden*, the work seems new to me every time I reread it, then it fits my definition of great. And I am constantly on the lookout for more great American works to add to my list.

Living with an author has a special meaning for me. It means that over a period of years my search will include all of that author's work, as well as everything written about the author. For Mark Twain that includes thirty volumes published before he died and at least a dozen published later, a dozen biographies, a dozen critical works, and over a thousand articles (critical, historical, or biographical) published in scholarly journals.

Such a reading program is just for starters. One cannot hope to write a scholarly article about an author unless one reads—and knows—everything previously written that has even the slightest relation to the topic.

You probably get the picture. A professor lives with an author for several years, reading and rereading, and emerges with a sense of the author's style and an understanding of the author's character that are imprinted for life.

Now multiply by twenty or so major American authors, starting with Edgar Allan Poe in the 1830s and moving to such contemporaries as Alice Walker or Toni Morrison. Add a few dozen less-than-major American authors, such as Harriet Beecher Stowe or Mary Wilkins Freeman, and one can see why so much time must be devoted to reading.

And rereading too, for it is difficult to find a new slant for the classroom without making a fresh rereading. Is there anything fresh left to discover after twenty or thirty rereadings? Almost always. Why? Because one cannot step into a moving stream twice. The reader's life changes: The perception of single people in their mid-twenties is not the same perception of two decades later with perhaps a spouse, children, and mid-career shoals to navigate; and that perception will likely differ again decades later as grandchildren and a ripening maturity enrich a life.

And the eras change. The upheaval-filled sixties were not the same as the conservative years that followed. Furthermore, the avalanche of new critical approaches continues to engulf readers. Early in the century and even later there was a great hue and cry about Freud's theories of infant sexuality, meaning that every work could now be reread in the light of such analytical symbols as the id, the ego, and the libido. Contests between mother and daughter or father and son could now be attributed to the Oedipus complex. And so the secrets of human motivation could be unlocked and the mysteries of human behavior explained—or so the Freudians and later the Jungians thought, though many disagreed.

Many decades later the feminist approach achieved prominence, meaning one could now read *Huck Finn* to try to understand Twain's treatment of women. Or one could read Flannery O'Connor, Eudora Welty, or Tillie Olsen to discover how the role of women has changed or to gain insight into the problems and difficulties women face.

What will the next new approach be? It is too hazardous to predict, but one can be sure that there will continue to be new analytical tools for dissecting and discussion.

And there will be new kinds of fiction, too. The short story—often the proving ground for fiction—has been caught in the throes of innovation for decades: plotless and characterless stories or mental puzzles set by the authors for the readers to solve if they wish. Now the trend is away from such innovation toward new ways of revealing and illuminating character. But as always, character depiction and character change in the light of the pressures and trials of the current era will be the staple of fiction.

As you can see, everything changes and everything stays the same. And so it will be for readers. Reading and rereading will continue to be the tried-and-true method of knowing what has changed and what will endure.

Salinger's *The Catcher in the Rye,* for instance, is, when read four decades after publication, almost a completely different book. Why? Because Holden Caulfield's dissatisfaction with the adult society of his day—a discontent perhaps shared by many in the early 1950s—is not typical of current youthful anxieties, nor is today's adult society identical to the one he rebelled against.

Rereading your own list of favorites has at least three advantages: (1) it allows you to see how much you (or your taste in books) has changed; (2) it allows you to see how much changes in the spirit of the times have altered your understanding of the book; and finally, (3) rereaders (if I may so name them) are much more likely to discover new standards of judgment to apply to contemporary authors and to set up new personal guidelines for all-time favorites. In other words, rereading allows readers to etch into their consciousnesses what it is to be alive and human.

Perhaps a sensible summary of the advantages of rereading is implied in Mark Twain's comment on how one's perspective changes. Twain said, "When I was a boy of fourteen, my father was so ignorant I could hardly stand to have the old man around. But when I got to be twenty-one I was astonished how much he had learned in seven years."

Average rate on Chapter 22: over 500 wpm. Turn to the Comprehension Check on page 131.

Application Exercise: Chapter 22

Using Self-knowledge and a Crystal Ball

Read each of the following passages and write two or three sentences on how a reader like yourself would have reacted to it three or more years ago. Then do the same on how you would react thirty years from now. Note that the exercise calls for both self-knowledge and a crystal ball. Names of authors and dates of publication are deliberately omitted.

1. It was the best of times, it was the worst of times, it was the age of wisdom, it was the age of foolishness, it was the epoch of belief, it was the epoch of incredulity, it was the season of Light, it was the season of Darkness, it was the spring of hope, it was the winter of despair, we had everything before us, we had nothing before us, we were all going direct to Heaven, we were all going direct the other way—in short, the period was so far like the present period, that some of its noisiest authorities insisted on its being received, for good or for evil, in the superlative degree of comparison only.

2. I met a traveler from an antique land,
Who said: Two vast and trunkless legs of stone
Stand in the desert. Near them, on the sand,
Half sunk, a shattered visage lies, whose frown,
And wrinkled lip, and sneer of cold command,
Tell that its sculptor well those passions read,
Which yet survive, stamped on these lifeless things,
The hand that mocked them, and the heart that fed:
And on the pedestal these words appear:
"My name is Ozymandias, King of Kings:
Look on my works, you Mighty, and despair!"
Nothing beside remains. Round the decay
Of that colossal wreck, boundless and bare,
The lone and level sands stretch far away.

3. Then two harlots came to the king, and stood before him. The one woman said, "Oh my lord, this woman and I dwell in the same house; and I gave birth to a child while she was in the house. Then on the third day after I was delivered, this woman also gave birth; and we were alone; there was no one else with us in the house, only we two were in the house. And this woman's son died in the night because she lay on

it. And she arose at midnight, and took my son from beside me, while your maidservant slept, and laid it in her bosom, and laid her dead son in my bosom. When I rose in the morning to nurse my child, behold, it was dead; but when I looked at it closely in the morning, behold, it was not the child that I had borne." But the other woman said, "No, the living child is mine, and the dead child is yours." The first said, "No, the dead child is yours, and the living child is mine." Thus they spake before the king.

Then the king said, "The one says, 'This is my son that is alive, and your son is dead'; and the other says, 'No, but your son is dead, and my son is the living one.' " And the king said, "Bring me a sword." So a sword was brought before the king. And the king said, "Divide the living child in two, and give half to the one and half to the other." Then the woman whose son was alive said to the king, because her heart yearned for her son, "Oh, my lord, give her the living child, and by no means slay it." But the other said, "It shall be neither mine nor yours; divide it." Then the king answered and said, "Give the living child to the first woman, and by no means slay it; she is its mother." And all Israel heard of the judgment which the king had rendered; and they stood in awe of the king, because they perceived that the wisdom of God was in him, to render justice.

4. Unless <u>wariness</u> be used, as good almost kill a man as kill a good book. Who kills a man kills a reasonable creature, God's image; but he who destroys a good book, kills reason itself, kills the image of God, as it were in the eye. Many a man lives a burden to the earth; but a good book is the precious life-blood of a master spirit, <u>embalmed</u> and treasured up on purpose to a life beyond life.

5. No man is an island entire of itself; every man is a piece of the continent, a part of the main. If a clod be washed away by the sea, Europe is the less, as well as if a <u>promontory</u> were, as well as if a manor of thy friend's or of thine own were. Any man's death diminishes me, because I am involved in mankind, and therefore never send to know for whom the bell tolls; it tolls for thee.

23 Playing with Words

Let's take a breather from the serious tone of the previous chapters and talk about the fun of playing with words. After all, you can read humorous material for speed too, right?

The world is divided into two kinds of people: those who take their pleasure from playing with words and those who don't. The latter may place a supreme value on words as a practical matter, but they don't revel in words or search with eye and ear in odd corners of their reading for new examples of something outlandish and delightful.

Perhaps it depends on a sense of humor—and while few people would claim to lack a funny bone, there is a humor that is cultivated in a special way. Some would say that people who love puns have a peculiar or "punny" sense of humor, and those of us who use puns frequently—indeed, we create opportunities to work them in—are willing to suffer the slings and arrows of outraged listeners to satisfy our abnormal craving for word play. Whatever the source of the urge, we can all use our reading time, whether for utilitarian purposes or for enrichment, to deepen our pleasure in the twists and double meanings of English.

One list comes from reading material that was meant to be serious, but in its effort to add tone, hit the wrong key. In a plumbing catalog, for instance, a $700 toilet has a "flush actuator" instead of a handle, and a greeting card company sells cards and "related social expression merchandise." Nothing is intrinsically wrong with these phrases, of course, but they seem to clog the channel instead of opening it. Since they trip over their own feet, they are funny. Word fanciers hoard such examples, and clogged thinking, for better or for worse, seems to be saturating us.

Another category of humor in word play is, at least in the history of humor, a fairly recent development. It is the bumper sticker that portrays both ignorance and outrage at the same time. Bumper stickers? Well, word play is where you find it, right? To distinguish the special sticker from the run-of-the-mill "Vote-for-George" variety, I call the playful kind "bumpernyms," using the "nym" part from association with synonym and antonym, where "nym" means word. Examples of bumpernyms are: "Stop continental drift," and "Stamp out temper tantrums."

Perhaps the world's greatest humorist was Mark Twain, whose specialty was word play, demonstrated in quick one-liners and in stories that bubbled along, deliberately misleading the reader into thinking something would happen. A good example of the latter in his story of Jim Blaine's grandfather's old ram, a tale that percolates for fifteen minutes when it is performed on the stage, and the further it moves from the climax the funnier it is. He tells of Jim's grandfather buying a ram and climbing the fence to inspect it the next day. A dime dropped out of his pocket when his back was to the ram, and he bent over to pick it up, fumbling in the grass, the ram heading toward him at forty miles an hour, with Smith of Calavaras watching; no, it was Smith of Tulare; no, it was Smith of Sacramento, who married a Whitaker, who gave a glass eye to Flora Ann Baxter, who married a Hagadorn, who was eaten by cannibals, but not by accident, as the example of Uncle Lem's dog shows, a dog he got from Wheeler, who was caught up in the machinery of the carpet factory. Since we never hear what happened after the ram headed for Jim's grandfather, the story is a successful exercise in sustained suspense, and is, in fact, a hoax on the listener.

But isn't all humor something of a hoax on the reader or listener? The factor that makes humor work is a reversal of expectations or a substituting of one thing for another. So the ram story, with all its apparently aimless rambling, is just a larger example of the essence of word play, where one thing substitutes for another.

Twain's delight in word play is illustrated in his one-liners. "Ignorant people think it's the noise which fighting cats make that is so aggravating, but it ain't so; it's the sickening grammar they use." Another: "In the first place God made idiots. This was for practice. Then he made school boards." And just one more: "It could probably be shown by facts and figures that there is no distinctively American criminal class—except Congress." Note that Twain is cleverly substituting an unexpected word in his one-liners. We don't expect to see idiots and school boards mentioned in the same sentence; nor do we think of cats using grammar nor of people in Congress called criminals. At least it isn't our normal expectation of the Congress. These instances show Twain having fun with words and sharing a special delight with the reader. In these one-liners he is out for a direct laugh, and so skilled was he on the stage that he always got it, but sometimes in his writing he buried a joke in the middle of a beautiful descriptive paragraph, as in the line, "a solitary esophagus swept on motionless wing." One reads that and moves on without thinking until suddenly the thought occurs—how can an esophagus fly? Twain has dipped into his humor well and zapped us.

A final example of word play, surely one of the sweetest delights of a wide-ranging reading program, is the two-time Bulwer-Lytton contest held by San Jose State University. The contest sought to find the funniest opening sentence from the worst novels ever written, and the following sentence, while not among the ten thousand entries, is an example of language run seriously amok. "It was summer, and the clouds stretched tight across the horizon, as they did almost every summer (except in 1988 when they perched on each other's wispy shoulders) like a prisoner stretching many fingers through the bars for a hack saw, even though there were no bars or saws, as Julia sniffed soulfully and slouched wearily toward the animal shelter."

Average rate for Chapter 23: over 500 wpm. Turn to the Comprehension Check on page 132.

Application Exercise: Chapter 23

Explaining What's Funny

Various kinds of humor are often found in combination with one another, making it difficult to isolate what's funny. Read this list of some kinds and elements of humor, and be prepared to use the terms to identify kinds or elements of humor in the examples that follow.

1. Puns. Sometimes it isn't punny. "The chef always delivers a 'State of the Onion' speech on New Year's Day."
2. Using an inflated or overly profound term for an everyday item, thus pricking the balloon of pomposity. The "flush-actuator" is an example.
3. Reversal of expectations. When we read that God made idiots, we don't expect to hear about school boards next.
4. Substituting one thing for another. Examples are "solitary esophagus " or the one-liner about the grammar of cats.
5. Exaggeration. Examples are the 114 literary mistakes in Cooper's novel, or Paul Bunyan stories that tell about Babe, the blue ox, whose stride was so long it took two people standing close together to see from one hoof print to the next.
6. Irreverence. To paraphrase Mark Twain, "There is no criminal class—except Congress."
7. Juxtaposition. This consists of placing unlike things next to one another, for example, placing a tall person next to a short one, mixing the beautiful (a rose) with the ugly (a compost pile), or showing the fast (rabbit) with the slow (turtle).

Using the above list, explain what is funny about the following Mark Twain items. Note that not all the terms on the list are used and that some are combined with others.

1. "A classic is something that everybody wants to have read and nobody wants to read."
2. "The reports of my death are greatly exaggerated."
3. "When in doubt, tell the truth."
4. "By trying, we can easily learn to endure adversity. Another man's, I mean."
5. "Now and then we had a hope that if we lived and were good, God would permit us to be pirates."
6. "Training is everything. The peach was once a bitter almond; cauliflower is nothing but cabbage with a college education."
7. "I'd rather decline four drinks than one German noun."

Vocabulary in Context III

These words have been selected from the Application Exercises for Chapter 16 through 23. Match the words with their definition by writing the number of each word next to its definition. The Answer Key is on page 135.

Words from Chapters 16 and 19

1.	disposition	_____ tyranny
2.	vexed	_____ upset
3.	foppery	_____ declare sacred
4.	in countenance	_____ in favor with
5.	incorrigible	_____ safe and sober way
6.	consecrate	_____ overconcern with appearance
7.	unalienable	_____ handling
8.	prudence	_____ acts of taking over
9.	usurpations	_____ not able to change
10.	despotism	_____ cannot be separated

Words from Chapter 20

1.	decorous	_____ continuously
2.	personages	_____ proper
3.	relevancy	_____ shun or avoid
4.	crass	_____ human beings
5.	persistently	_____ excess verbiage
6.	eschew	_____ artful devices
7.	surplusage	_____ coarse, stupid
8.	artifices	_____ related to matter at hand

Words from Chapter 21

1.	brooded	_____ changing
2.	immortal	_____ meditated
3.	transmuting	_____ reproached
4.	imperishableness	_____ poisonous
5.	noxious	_____ cannot be destroyed
6.	incursions	_____ those who correct
7.	disparaged	_____ those with an excessive love of books
8.	emendators	_____ never dying
9.	bibliomaniacs	_____ inroads

Words from Chapters 22 and 23

1.	epoch	_____ hardship, misfortune
2.	incredulity	_____ face
3.	visage	_____ women of ill repute
4.	sneer	_____ tube from throat area to stomach
5.	harlots	_____ disbelief
6.	wariness	_____ scornful facial expression
7.	embalmed	_____ period of time
8.	promontory	_____ act of placing side by side for contrast
9.	esophagus	_____ caution
10.	juxtaposition	_____ high land jutting out to sea
11.	adversity	_____ preserved in memory

MASTER VOCABULARY LIST

The words on the following list come from the three *Vocabulary in Context* exercises, which may be found on pages 20, 47, and 103. If you have learned the meanings of the words in the three exercises cited, it should not be difficult to check your memory by writing the meanings after each word here. These words are taken from the Application Exercises and not from the chapters themselves. When in doubt about a word, check its meaning in a dictionary.

accessible
actuated
adversity
affection
ailment
alma mater
analogy
artifice
assumption
bibliomaniac
breach
brood
cohere
confute
consecrate
consciousness
crass
cyclical
decorous
despotism
disparaged
disposition
embalmed
emendator
entity
epic
epoch
eschew
esophagus

extract
folly
forlorn
foppery
goad
hallow
harlot
humor
immortal
impediment
imperishableness
impressionistic
incorrigible
incountenance
incredulity
incursions
in medias res
juxtaposition
latterly
linear sequence
marshaling
metabolism
mythological
nomenclature
noxious
persistent
personage
pervert (v.)
practitioner

preconceived
pre-established
promontory
provoked
prudence
pruning
puny
reciprocal
relevancy
relinquish
reparation
restitution
revenge
sloth
sneer
squalid
subjective
surplusage
titular
transmuting
unaffected
unalienable
usurpation
vexed
visage
wariness
wit
wrought out

24 Choosing Your Reading

Throughout this book you have been learning to become a skillful reader. You have found out how to overcome your bad reading habits by forcing good ones to take their place. You have some knowledge about various reading skills, from skimming to training in comprehension—knowledge that is important because it helps you to become an efficient reader. But the teaching of efficient reading is not the only purpose of this book. By learning how to read better you should have a strong desire to read more—more good books.

One university's recommended list of novels contains works by more than 260 authors. At the rate of one a week, it would take five years to read one book per author. So we are forced to be selective. Knowing it is impossible to read all we would like to, our concern is to choose the best.

Useful publications to turn to in a search for the best contemporary books are the major magazines and the Sunday book review sections of large metropolitan newspapers. The Sunday book review section of the *New York Times* is perhaps the most generally available. In these publications you will find critical comments by qualified reviewers on books published during the week. The business of the reviewers is to read a new book, digest it, and tell the world whether or not it is worth reading, in their opinion.

Reviews in current newspapers and magazines are valuable for criticism of the latest books. Suppose, however, you pick up a book on a topic that interests you, *Penetrating the Mind*, published a number of years ago, and you wish to find out what the critical opinion of the book is. A useful publication, the *Book Review Digest* will serve your purpose. Of course, you could read back copies of a single magazine that reviews books weekly or monthly, but the *Book Review Digest*, which provides a selection of critical opinion from all the important sources of reviews, is a much more convenient instrument to use. Each year a large selection of book reviews on every subject is included in this publication. You need only to find the volume for the year in which *Penetrating the Mind* was published to learn what the favorable and unfavorable opinions were. The *Book Review Digest* attempts to present a cross section of opinion, usually limited to brief comments that indicate each critic's capsule opinion of the book.

For contemporary books, then, see the criticisms in the magazines, the Sunday *New York Times*, or the *Book Review Digest*. For the best books among the classics, turn to those recommended in the paperback book,

Good Reading, which was published under the authority of the National Council of Teachers of English. Many of these recommended books will provide you with stimulating reading. To be sure, there are very few adventure stories or "whodunits" on their list, but the *Good Reading* guide, as well as books chosen by the Great Books Foundation, includes books that will set you to thinking more deeply than you usually do when you read. A sure mark of educated persons is their familiarity with the ideas in the great books.

Remember that the popularity of a book does not indicate its greatness. And unless it concerns some controversial matter, its popularity may not even make it a worthy topic of conversation. It is foolish, therefore, to read the most popular books on the best-seller list just to have something to talk about. It happens, unfortunately, that a number of them don't amount to very much in the long run. If you were to review the best sellers for the past fifty years, you would find that many of the most popular have been forgotten. For example, the novels of authors like E. P. Roe and Mrs. E.D.E.N. Southworth, which were best sellers at the turn of the century, are very seldom mentioned in any of the surveys of our literary culture. There are books for the hour and books for the ages. If you value your time, choose wisely when you select your literary company.

The great books of our own age, those that have exerted a profound influence on our time, are very few. Even if you have not read them, you should be aware of the force and power of such books as the Bible and the works of Charles Darwin, Karl Marx, and Sigmund Freud. In these books you will find ideas that form the nucleus of the molding forces of our age.

Members of the advisory board of *Good Reading* submitted a personal list of basic books that they would buy first if their libraries were somehow destroyed. Many of the old favorites, such as Shakespeare, the Bible, Homer, Plato, Montaigne, Tolstoy, and Melville, were mentioned, but it is interesting to note that H. G. Wells's *Outline of History* was listed as frequently as many of the others in this sampling of the literary sympathies of modern American writers. The lists were drawn up by contemporary authors, critics, and poets—people of broad culture and cultivated taste; and if these books proved "basic" to them, they ought to prove good reading for us.

Choose your books as you would choose your friends: Have a speaking acquaintance with many; be on intimate terms with a few; be on the lookout for new ones and hold fast to the old ones you have found worthy. Some books, like some people, are not worth knowing well. Usually it is not necessary to be with bad people long to know what they are like. Neither is it necessary to read a poor book all the way through. Some books, like some friends, are worth visiting frequently; we never cease to enjoy their company.

Choose your books wisely and read them well. Enter the world of books with an open, inquiring mind, and it will share with you a wealth that is beyond measuring.

Good reading to you!

Average rate for Chapter 24: over 500 wpm. Turn to the Comprehension Check on page 133.

Application Exercise: Chapter 24

Recalling What's Happened

Allow ten minutes for this test covering important points in *Reading Skills*. In front of each item write *T* for true or *F* for false. Each of the *ten* true items counts ten points, and a perfect score is 100. The Answer Key is on page 136.

1. In college about 15 percent of all study activity involves the reading process.
2. If you are reading over 200 words per minute, the chances are you are a word-by-word reader.
3. You need not worry about straining your eyes by reading at very rapid rates unless you wear glasses.
4. A good reading distance for most people is fourteen to sixteen inches from the eyes.
5. Most good books these days are printed on bright, white paper and in clear, black type.
6. A reader makes a regression when he tries to translate a single word into a meaningful idea.
7. The number of fixations depends on the difficulty of the material and not the purpose of the reader.
8. The amount of time spent in moving the eyes is about the same amount needed to make fixations.
9. *Reading Skills* can provide success without mechanical devices except for a watch.
10. You should use a constant rate when reading a textbook in order to understand each section equally well.
11. The signposts of a book refer only to chapter headings and subheadings.
12. Doctors have determined with scientific accuracy how habits are formed.
13. Learning words in context is the best and easiest way to improve your vocabulary.
14. Because reading is an important study aid, all reading habits should be kept, even at the cost of breaking others.
15. The two main kinds of vocabulary are: (1) vocabulary of a textbook and (2) vocabulary of a newspaper.
16. The dictionary usually establishes one standard meaning for a word.
17. The average reading rate for adults is 250 to 300 words per minute.
18. People have been known to read 4000 words per minute.
19. If you set up a reading program for yourself, plan to spend at least two to four hours a day on it.
20. It is sufficient to practice increasing your rate of reading by spending one full period a week on it.
21. A successful reading-rate improvement program can be accomplished in a month or two.
22. In an outline the main ideas are usually set off by Arabic numerals.
23. It is not a good idea—in fact, it is illogical—to look at the conclusion of the section or chapter before beginning to read it.

24. Skimming by an automatic or mechanical process (e.g., reading every fourth page) is particularly efficient.
25. If you have a question in mind and, using the index and chapter headings, read to find the answer, you will be skimming well.
26. When you skim you read everything faster than usual.
27. It is inefficient to skim a whole magazine before reading it thoroughly.
28. It is important to read groups of words; never, even on a crucial passage, examine each word as you read.
29. The supreme test of skillful readers is their ability to read critically and creatively.
30. A poor reader often makes four to five fixations per line.
31. Forcing yourself to read more carefully will make it possible to turn hearing into seeing.
32. In a reading program to increase rate, you read just beyond your comfortable rate.
33. Too often a book becomes messy and less useful if you write in it.
34. When taking notes, it is usually best to jot down direct quotations.
35. A good summary includes all the facts and examples that prove the author's point.
36. The only real standard of an author's language should be the degree of its clarity.
37. If you write only the concluding sentences of an article, you will have a fair summary of its contents.
38. Poetry should be read silently and with deep thought, not emotionally.
39. The analytical approach of feminists is not appropriate to reading *Huck Finn*.
40. When you read a work of great literature for the first time, you should relax and read for sheer enjoyment.
41. It is better to have chosen the wrong theme or unifying principle of a book as you are reading it than to choose none at all.
42. The opinions of astute professional critics determine whether a book is good or bad or somewhere between good and bad.
43. When you dissect a book part by part, you destroy some of the beauty of the whole and the impact of its unity.
44. It is possible and often desirable when analyzing to state the theme of a very long book in a dozen words or so.
45. A reader who constantly challenges the author's purpose in putting one part of a book before another gains understanding but loses aesthetic enjoyment.
46. The public library, because it is widely used, has a tremendous impact on American life.
47. *The Reader's Guide to Periodical Literature* issues a bi-annual index of most of the magazines in America.
48. The first step in looking up a topic in the library would normally be to go to the call desk.
49. Those who read well orally usually cannot read as well silently.
50. Transferring the rate of your oral reading to silent reading will strengthen your ability to read silently.

Comprehension Checks

Write the letters of the best answers in the blanks. Answer Key appears on page 136.

1. In college, the percentage of all study activity involving the reading process is:
    (a) 50%   (c) 75%
    (b) 85%   (d) 65%   _____

2. To learn to comprehend better you should learn to read:
    (a) each word separately   (c) in whole phrases
    (b) each symbolically   (d) none of these   _____

3. If you read much it is important to:
    (a) have your glasses checked regularly
    (b) wear your glasses only when reading
    (c) wear reading glasses
    (d) glasses not mentioned   _____

4. It is true that when you read fast:
    (a) you cannot comprehend as accurately
    (b) you cannot retain as long
    (c) you can understand as much as when you read slowly
    (d) none of these   _____

5. Skillful reading requires:
    (a) good illumination   (c) efficient eye movements
    (b) good reading environment   (d) none of these mentioned _____

6. Formal teaching of reading usually ceases after:
    (a) elementary grades   (c) senior high grades
    (b) junior high grades   (d) subject not mentioned   _____

7. You may infer from this chapter that an important aspect of reading is the reader's:
    (a) past experience   (c) perception of the author
    (b) span of reading   (d) sensitivity   _____

8. Performance in rational learning:
    (a) increases with maturity   (c) has no effect on reading
    (b) decreases with maturity   (d) subject not mentioned   _____

9. When you read you should:
    (a) keep in mind the main idea
    (b) relate important items to the main idea
    (c) draw a conclusion and relate your reading to your background
    (d) do all of these things   _____

10. The efficient reader reads faster than:
    (a) 500 wpm (words per minute)   (c) 2000 wpm
    (b) 100 wpm   (d) subject not mentioned _____

110

Write the letters of the best answers in the blanks. Answer Key appears on page 136.

1. Your reading habits are conditioned by:
   (a) physical attributes   (c) personality factors
   (b) mental skills   (d) all of these   _____

2. A word-by-word reader probably reads slower than:
   (a) 100 wpm   (c) 200 wpm
   (b) 150 wpm   (d) subject not mentioned   _____

3. Eliminate lip reading by:
   (a) thrusting a pencil between your teeth
   (b) sticking a knuckle in your mouth
   (c) neither of these
   (d) either of these   _____

4. The reading skill that can be developed very quickly is:
   (a) vocabulary   (c) speed
   (b) comprehension   (d) eye movements   _____

5. Vocabulary can be improved by:
   (a) alertness and ability to concentrate
   (b) drill, discipline, and practice
   (c) testing frequently
   (d) subject not mentioned   _____

6. You can become conscious of pronouncing each word in your throat by:
   (a) looking at yourself in a mirror
   (b) having a friend watch you read
   (c) feeling your throat with your fingers
   (d) none of these   _____

7. For the most part comprehension depends on:
   (a) drill, discipline, and practice on magazine articles
   (b) alertness and the ability to concentrate
   (c) reading at a good speed; avoiding word-by-word reading
   (d) none of these   _____

8. You cannot read well if you:
   (a) read in bed
   (b) listen to the radio at the same time
   (c) read in a moving vehicle
   (d) none of these mentioned   _____

9. This chapter deals mainly with:
   (a) obstacles in the path of efficient reading
   (b) how to survey your reading habits
   (c) how to increase your speed of reading
   (d) none of these   _____

10. You may infer from this chapter that a survey of your present reading habits is:
    (a) far more   (c) far less
    (b) slightly more   (d) slightly less   _____
    important in a reading efficiency program than making a determined effort to increase the amount of reading you do.

Write the letters of the best answers in the blanks. Answer Key appears on page 136.

1. This chapter is mainly about:
   (a) reading hazards
   (b) keeping in good shape for skillful reading
   (c) how to take care of your eyes while reading
   (d) none of these _____

2. The best kind of paper for printed matter is:
   (a) dull white   (c) pure white
   (b) shiny white   (d) none of these _____

3. In general, the health of your eyes ordinarily depends on:
   (a) your diet
   (b) eye exercises
   (c) the overall health of your body
   (d) proper care of your visual organs _____

4. You should have your eyes checked:
   (a) before you begin school
   (b) when you enter an occupation that requires close reading
   (c) at regular intervals
   (d) both *b* and *c* _____

5. Some people have become dizzy when reading:
   (a) aboard ships   (c) in taxicabs
   (b) in an airplane   (d) none of these mentioned _____

6. The best position for a book you are reading is:
   (a) flat on the table or desk   (c) in an inclined position
   (b) upright in your hand   (d) not mentioned _____

7. When reading, avoid a strained or twitching feeling about the eyes by:
   (a) looking at some distant object from time to time
   (b) massaging the eyes carefully
   (c) getting glasses to correct defects of vision
   (d) none of these mentioned _____

8. Most people hold a book so that the distance from the eyes is:
   (a) 11 to 13 inches   (c) 17 to 19 inches
   (b) 14 to 16 inches   (d) none of these mentioned _____

9. People who read eight or more hours a day have no eye fatigue because they:
   (a) concentrate intensively   (c) read rapidly, in whole phrases
   (b) are used to reading   (d) none of these mentioned _____

10. When you try to read yourself to sleep you:
    (a) ruin your eyes
    (b) relax too much
    (c) break training rules for efficient reading
    (d) none of these mentioned _____

Write the letters of the best answers in the blanks. Answer Key appears on page 136.

1. The eyes move across a line of print:
   (a) in one smooth, even movement
   (b) by going backward and forward
   (c) in starts and stops
   (d) none of these _____

2. The number of fixations a slow reader makes per line is:
   (a) 10 to 12
   (b) 15 to 17
   (c) 3 to 5
   (d) none of these _____

3. The amount of time spent moving the eyes as compared to the amount of time to make a fixation is:
   (a) shorter
   (b) the same
   (c) longer
   (d) subject not mentioned _____

4. One of the best ways to improve eye movements is to practice:
   (a) on an eye-exercise sheet
   (b) on an instrument
   (c) reading light, interesting material
   (d) none of these _____

5. Regressions are caused by:
   (a) eyestrain
   (b) poor illumination
   (c) twitching eyes
   (d) none of these mentioned _____

6. In comparison to the first page, the class of freshmen who read the second page in half the time:
   (a) concentrated almost as intensively
   (b) improved their eye movements
   (c) remembered almost as much
   (d) concentrated much more intensively _____

7. The number of fixations depends upon:
   (a) the difficulty of the material
   (b) the purpose of the reader
   (c) both of these
   (d) neither of these _____

8. When readers, like typists, begin to consider individual words, they:
   (a) become less efficient
   (b) become more painstaking
   (c) make fewer errors
   (d) subject not mentioned _____

9. When you read familiar material over and over again against time, you:
   (a) become bored with it
   (b) see new meanings
   (c) see new, logical groupings of words
   (d) subject not mentioned _____

10. You will be able to read more efficiently if you:
    (a) are conscious of eye movements
    (b) exercise your eyes diligently
    (c) apply both of these
    (d) neither of these _____

Write the letters of the best answers in the blanks. Answer Key appears on page 136.

1. The main idea of this chapter is:
   (a) concentrate intensively   (c) read rapidly
   (b) comprehend accurately   (d) none of these   _____

2. You read slowly a technical work on a subject with which you are not very familiar because you need to:
   (a) absorb the style   (c) learn new vocabulary
   (b) take notes   (d) both b and c   _____

3. When you read for enrichment of life, you read:
   (a) with undivided attention   (c) both of these
   (b) slowly and with caution   (d) subject not mentioned   _____

4. When you read for the author's general trend of thought, you read:
   (a) rapidly   (c) both of these
   (b) slowly and carefully   (d) subject not mentioned   _____

5. If you tried to read a number of biographies of any one person, you would:
   (a) read them all slowly
   (b) read the last ones more rapidly
   (c) read them all rapidly
   (d) subject not mentioned   _____

6. To locate information on a historical figure in a large history book, you would:
   (a) read the whole book swiftly   (c) read the whole book slowly
   (b) use the glossary   (d) none of these   _____

7. Rapid reading helps decrease:
   (a) eyestrain   (c) both of these
   (b) twitching eyes   (d) subject not mentioned   _____

8. The term *shifting gears*, as used in this chapter, refers to changing:
   (a) degree of concentration   (c) speed of reading
   (b) the purpose of your reading   (d) none of these   _____

9. You may assume from reading this chapter that:
   (a) there is no correct speed of reading
   (b) reading is strictly individual
   (c) both of these
   (d) neither of these   _____

10. A popularized version of your topic allows you to:
    (a) shift into low   (c) coast along
    (b) shift into second   (d) subject not mentioned   _____

Comprehension Check: Chapter 6

Write the letters of the best answers in the blanks. Answer Key appears on page 136.

1. The chief rule for skimming is:
    (a) move rapidly   (c) read for a purpose
    (b) comprehend accurately (d) none of these   _____

2. To find specific information listed in the *World Almanac*, turn first to the:
    (a) index   (c) either of these
    (b) table of contents   (d) none of these   _____

3. The sports page of a newspaper usually:
    (a) follows the business section (c) is in the same location
    (b) follows the comics   (d) subject not mentioned   _____

4. The publication that lends itself most readily to skimming is the:
    (a) pamphlet   (c) popular novel
    (b) newspaper   (d) subject not mentioned   _____

5. You can get a good clue to a magazine story's plot by:
    (a) looking at the pictures   (c) neither of these
    (b) reading the subtitles   (d) subject not mentioned   _____

6. Skimming a book is like:
    (a) skimming a flat rock over   (c) both of these
        water
    (b) skimming cream off milk   (d) neither of these   _____

7. The publication that prints all the news that's fit to print is:
    (a) the *New York Times*   (c) the *Christian Science Monitor*
    (b) the *Chicago Tribune*   (d) publication not
                                  mentioned   _____

8. You skim when you are reading:
    (a) the headlines   (c) the picture page
    (b) the comics   (d) none of these   _____

9. Important items to efficient skimmers are:
    (a) chapter headings   (c) both of these
    (b) subheadings   (d) neither of these   _____

10. You can infer from reading this chapter that in normal reading (that is, not skimming) you:
    (a) read word for word   (c) do not omit portions
    (b) group words   (d) none of these   _____

Write the letters of the best answers in the blanks. Answer Key appears on page 136.

1. This chapter is mainly about:
   (a) good comprehension   (c) both of these
   (b) rapid reading   (d) neither of these   _____

2. A good illustration of reading intensively is offered by readers of:
   (a) comic books   (c) long novels
   (b) scholarly essays   (d) none of these   _____

3. Cure yourself of daydreaming when you read by:
   (a) forcing yourself to read intensively
   (b) skipping a few pages
   (c) sleeping a little while
   (d) none of these   _____

4. One way to learn to concentrate is by:
   (a) reading the same material over and over
   (b) reading late at night
   (c) reading in the same place
   (d) none of these   _____

5. You may have difficulty concentrating if:
   (a) the lighting is bad   (c) both of these are true
   (b) your glasses need adjusting (d) neither of these
                                       mentioned   _____

6. To improve concentration:
   (a) read for a definite purpose (c) read to get out of a rut
   (b) read to broaden your   (d) none of these
       knowledge   _____

7. Two men who tried to concentrate in cork-lined chambers were:
   (a) Carlyle and Poe   (c) Carlyle and Proust
   (b) Poe and Chaucer   (d) Chaucer and Proust   _____

8. The principle factor in good concentration is:
   (a) good lighting and comfort   (c) a quiet place to work
   (b) self-discipline and   (d) none of these
       conditioning   _____

9. This chapter recommends that you learn to concentrate at:
   (a) a table in the public library (c) neither of these places
   (b) your desk in your study   (d) either of these places _____

10. This chapter suggests you read:
    (a) rapidly   (c) both of these
    (b) for comprehension   (d) neither of these
                                       mentioned   _____

Write the letters of the best answers in the blanks. Answer Key appears on page 136.

1. This chapter emphasizes:
   (a) discarding the unneeded and retaining the valuable
   (b) using the index or table of contents
   (c) using the preface or introduction
   (d) rereading and discussing a book   _____

2. Perhaps the difficulty of poor readers is that they:
   (a) fail to relate generalizations and details
   (b) read hesitatingly
   (c) read too rapidly
   (d) none of these   _____

3. The point made about the autistic child is that:
   (a) a therapy was found   (c) therapy is not a full answer
   (b) a therapy was not found   (d) there is no therapy   _____

4. The statement, "Youth, as a rule, has an immense reserve of strength," is a:
   (a) generalization   (c) supporting statement
   (b) rule   (d) subject not mentioned   _____

5. A paragraph topic sentence:
   (a) concludes a unit of   (c) is both of these
       development
   (b) begins a unit of development (d) is always the first
                                        sentence   _____

6. When readers, looking for particular information, have found the part of the book in which it is located, they can:
   (a) skim for key words   (c) both of these
   (b) subordinate less relevant facts (d) neither of these   _____

7. The sign of a successful executive is:
   (a) an empty wastebasket at the start of the day
   (b) a full wastebasket at the end of the day
   (c) both of these
   (d) neither of these   _____

8. To comprehend well you must be able to:
   (a) skim rapidly and concentrate (c) use your eyes intelligently
   (b) use the signpost technique   (d) none of these   _____

9. Rapid reading of light, interesting material helps:
   (a) improve eye movements   (c) both of these
   (b) concentration   (d) subject not mentioned   _____

10. You can infer that good comprehension depends upon:
    (a) mental alertness
    (b) ability to sift the chaff from the wheat
    (c) ability to use the signpost technique
    (d) all of these   _____

Write the letters of the best answers in the blanks. Answer Key appears on page 136.

1. Which university pioneered in reading programs?
   (a) Iowa   (c) Chicago
   (b) Harvard   (d) all of the above   _____

2. Tachistoscope means:
   (a) speed viewer   (c) eye-movement recorder
   (b) rate accelerator   (d) none of these   _____

3. Among mechanical aids to motivate reading speed are:
   (a) compact discs   (c) tape recorders
   (b) 16-mm films   (d) none of these   _____

4. The scrolling rate of the personal computer in the example varied from:
   (a) 150 to 2000 wpm   (c) 300 to 570 wpm
   (b) 250 to 1000 wpm   (d) none of these   _____

5. If you cannot read at the computer-assisted rate of 570 wpm, you should:
   (a) keep at it until you can   (c) reprogram the computer
   (b) try the slowest rate   (d) increase your rate off the
                                             machine until you near
                                             570   _____

6. The chapter suggests you should be able to read at least how fast before you try 570 wpm on the computer? Within:
   (a) 100 words   (c) 50 words
   (b) 200 words   (d) 250 words   _____

7. The important caution about computer-assisted reading is that you should *not*:
   (a) read when tired   (c) prepare material beforehand
   (b) read difficult material   (d) expect to read as fast off the
                                             machine   _____

8. After reading on a computer you should go to practice reading when?
   (a) the very next day   (c) immediately
   (b) within a few hours   (d) subject not mentioned   _____

9. This chapter suggests that to obtain reading matter to use on a computer, you should:
   (a) develop you own material   (c) buy material beforehand
   (b) exchange material with   (d) none of these
       another person   _____

10. The 16-mm reading films increase on the order of what rate from one film to the next?
   (a) 50 wpm   (c) 150 wpm
   (b) 100 wpm   (d) 200 wpm   _____

Write the letters of the best answers in the blanks. Answer Key appears on page 136.

1. Habits are:
   (a) begun by a stimulus
   (b) formed by impulses traveling to a nerve center
   (c) well-trod paths formed by impulses
   (d) all of these   _____

2. Nerve impulses begin by:
   (a) unknown causes   (c) fluctuating rapidly
   (b) inherited characteristics   (d) subject not mentioned   _____

3. You keep habits:
   (a) because you can't get rid of them
   (b) unless you have reason to change
   (c) neither of these
   (d) subject not mentioned   _____

4. Habits:
   (a) make movements exact   (c) both of these
   (b) lessen fatigue   (d) neither of these
            mentioned   _____

5. A child learning to tie shoelaces illustrates:
   (a) trial-and-error method   (c) neither of these
   (b) a creature of habit   (d) subject not mentioned   _____

6. Habits that reduce the attention with which acts are performed:
   (a) are useful   (c) should be eliminated
   (b) are symptoms of carelessness   (d) both b and c   _____

7. Typical readers increased their number of words per minute from:
   (a) 400 to 800   (c) 250 to 850
   (b) 300 to 700   (d) 300 to 800   _____

8. Typical readers showed a big increase after the tenth or twelfth day because:
   (a) they had broken old habits   (c) both of these
   (b) they had formed new habits   (d) subject not mentioned   _____

9. If typical readers stopped practicing after the tenth period, they would:
   (a) soon revert to old habits
   (b) stay at that level
   (c) go beyond that level
   (d) none of these mentioned   _____

10. Typical readers succeeded because:
    (a) they had a strong desire to succeed
    (b) they practiced regularly
    (c) they made their habits automatic
    (d) all of these   _____

Match the following. Not all items in the left-hand column can be matched; none is used twice. Answer Key appears on page 136.

(a) thick, heavy lines
(b) this, that
(c) Dickens and Kipling
(d) stream of consciousness
(e) Woolf and Olsen
(f) first and last paragraphs
(g) used for afterthoughts
(h) Roman numerals
(i) for reference to one topic
(j) indicate contrast
(k) punctuation, type,
  and special words
(l) colon and semicolon
(m) Arabic numerals
(n) table of contents
(o) instrumentation

1. tricks of typography used by _____
2. italics sometimes used to show _____
3. boldface _____
4. reference words _____
5. dash _____
6. indicate main ideas in an outline _____
7. give idea of purpose _____
8. use the index _____
9. however, yet _____
10. mechanical aids _____

Comprehension Check: Chapter 12

Write the letters of the best answers in the blanks. Answer Key appears on page 136.

1. A dictionary will usually offer:
   (a) clues to context
   (b) one precise meaning for a word
   (c) clues to rapier words
   (d) a choice of meanings   _____

2. This chapter advises you to:
   (a) buy a dictionary
   (b) use a dictionary daily
   (c) learn new words from a dictionary
   (d) browse in a dictionary   _____

3. The best method of enriching your vocabulary is to:
   (a) learn words while reading
   (b) talk to many people
   (c) learn word lists
   (d) none of these   _____

4. Context means:
   (a) roots and prefixes of surrounding words
   (b) surrounding words which add to meaning
   (c) words that sound like one thing but mean something else
   (d) words used like synonyms   _____

5. The voters were confused about celibacy because they:
   (a) heard "accused" and "deliberately"
   (b) thought it meant "an unmarried state"
   (c) both of these
   (d) thought the senator a scoundrel   _____

6. Lincoln wrote to:
   (a) Horace Mann
   (b) Thomas Mann
   (c) Horace Greeley
   (d) none of these   _____

7. Everyone knows the final words of Patrick Henry's speech. The first ones are:
   (a) "Why stand we here idle?"
   (b) "Gentlemen may cry peace"
   (c) "Is life so dear or peace so sweet?"
   (d) "The war is actually begun"   _____

8. An important basis for judging people ought to be:
   (a) the size of their vocabulary
   (b) the equality of their vocabulary
   (c) their level of attainment
   (d) how actively they try to better themselves   _____

9. Words used as tools of criticism are:
   (a) rapier words
   (b) broadsword words
   (c) both of these
   (d) neither of these   _____

10. You will probably know how to use a word later if you learn it:
    (a) in a word list
    (b) in school or college
    (c) in context
    (d) none of these   _____

Write the letters of the best answers in the blanks. Answer Key appears on page 137.

1. The best notes are taken when you use:
   (a) pencil
   (b) ink
   (c) typewriter
   (d) none of these mentioned _____

2. This chapter suggests you take notes by:
   (a) using index cards
   (b) using a notebook
   (c) writing in the book
   (d) any and all of these _____

3. A method of note taking has gained popularity with the presence of the:
   (a) tape recorder
   (b) compact disc
   (c) video cassette recorder (VCR)
   (d) none of these _____

4. When you take notes in a book, it is a good idea to:
   (a) underline key statements
   (b) use colored pencils
   (c) write in the margin
   (d) all of these _____

5. A good general rule for note taking is to:
   (a) quote the author always
   (b) put it in your own words always
   (c) quote the author if it is put in a memorable way
   (d) write it in a memorable way yourself _____

6. When you take notes, record:
   (a) page number, author, and title
   (b) your location when you took notes
   (c) the time you took the notes
   (d) all of these _____

7. The form of your notes may be:
   (a) as an outline or summary
   (b) on different size cards
   (c) on different colored papers
   (d) all of these _____

8. When you take notes, concentrate on:
   (a) the author's organization
   (b) the author's phrasing
   (c) both of these
   (d) neither of these _____

9. Notes help you:
   (a) retain information
   (b) keep a permanent record
   (c) when giving a long and detailed speech before an audience
   (d) both a and b _____

10. When you take notes in the margin of a book, write a:
    (a) clear phrasing of a major topic
    (b) comment of your own
    (c) question the author failed to answer
    (d) any or all of these _____

Write the letters of the best answers in the blanks. Answer Key appears on page 137.

1. When you summarize, you must:
   (a) understand the main ideas and their relationship
   (b) record key points in connected form
   (c) choose an economical and exact method of expression
   (d) all of these _____

2. You will have a fair summary of an article if you write:
   (a) the first two paragraphs
   (b) the last two paragraphs
   (c) the topic sentence of each paragraph
   (d) the topic sentence of every third paragraph _____

3. When you write a summary for your own use, you:
   (a) abbreviate long words and leave out some short ones
   (b) omit dates and titles you already know
   (c) add implications of your own
   (d) all of these _____

4. The make good summaries, you must make decisions about:
   (a) the author's plan and key ideas
   (b) your purpose in the light of the author's purpose
   (c) the author's style of writing
   (d) all of these _____

5. An effective method of testing the worth of your summary is to:
   (a) try it out on a sympathetic friend
   (b) try it out on another book by the same author
   (c) set it aside for a month or two
   (d) none of these _____

6. You may infer that a summary should:
   (a) include all essential information
   (b) serve your purpose equally as well as the author's
   (c) include the entire last paragraph
   (d) both a and b _____

7. Many a young writer has been advised to:
   (a) live near the writer's best market, New York City
   (b) become more mature before attempting an ambitious work
   (c) let the material age
   (d) subject not mentioned _____

8. Your final summary should reflect clearly:
   (a) your opinion of the subject   (c) the wheat and the chaff
   (b) what the author said   (d) both b and c _____

9. A good example of a summary, according to this chapter, is a:
   (a) battle report of a general
   (b) policeman's report of an accident
   (c) student's summary of a term paper
   (d) none of these

10. Authors usually include a summary of their book:
   (a) on the dust jacket or cover   (c) in the introduction
   (b) in the preface   (d) none of these mentioned _____

Match the following. Not all the items in the left-hand column can be matched; none is used twice. Answer Key appears on page 137.

(a) subject, author, location
(b) *The Saturday Review* and *The Nation*
(c) date of publication
(d) table of contents
(e) call desk
(f) Englishmen
(g) card catalog or computer
(h) author, title, call number
(i) Union Catalog
(j) *The Atlantic* and *The Saturday Review*
(k) *Poole's Index to Periodical Literature*
(l) 10
(m) 20
(n) 48
(o) 70
(p) 90
(q) 100
(r) subject, title, author   _____
(s) *Harper's* and *The Atlantic*
(t) librarians
(u) publishers' list
(v) Kardex Visible File
(w) subject card
(x) *Newsweek* and *TV Guide*
(y) *The Reader's Guide to Periodical Literature*

1. What percentage of libraries were built by Carnegie?   _____
2. What percentage of people did not read a book in a three-year period?   _____
3. What lists each book in the library?   _____
4. Under what headings are books listed in the library?   _____
5. Where should investigation of magazines begin?   _____
6. What magazines are mentioned for a good analysis of a subject?   _____
7. What magazines are mentioned for a good popular treatment of a subject?   _____
8. Where do you look if you can't remember the author or title of a book?   _____
9. Over how many millions are strangers to the library?   _____
10. Who are critical of Americans?   _____

Write the letters of the best answers in the blanks. Answer Key appears on page 137.

1. This chapter states that doctors, because of their long training, are:
   (a) careful and analytical readers   (c) both of these
   (b) fast and skillful readers   (d) neither of these   _____

2. Find more time to read by organizing yourself and:
   (a) providing yourself with sufficient reading material
   (b) cutting out movies, television, and unnecessary activities
   (c) improving your reading habits
   (d) none of these   _____

3. Successful people, according to this chapter:
   (a) have little time for reading
   (b) travel widely and meet many people
   (c) have achieved financial goals
   (d) budget their time   _____

4. This chapter advises you not to:
   (a) read comics   (c) listen to daytime serials
   (b) watch television   (d) none of these   _____

5. The average rate of reading for adults is:
   (a) 100 to 150 wpm   (c) 200 to 250 wpm
   (b) 150 to 200 wpm   (d) 250 to 300 wpm   _____

6. A high school student read *The Good Earth* at:
   (a) 1200 wpm   (c) 800 wpm
   (b) 1000 wpm   (d) 600 wpm   _____

7. People have been known to read:
   (a) 600 wpm   (c) 800 wpm
   (b) 700 wpm   (d) over 900 wpm   _____

8. A number of people have increased their efficiency and doubled their reading rate in:
   (a) two weeks   (c) six weeks
   (b) four weeks   (d) eight weeks   _____

9. For most people, energy is at a low ebb:
   (a) an hour or so after arising
   (b) just before lunch
   (c) an hour or two before the evening meal
   (d) none of these   _____

10. You can infer from this chapter that a vacation from a reading program after the first week or two:
    (a) rests your eyes
    (b) allows a regression to old habits
    (c) conserves your energy
    (d) none of these   _____

Write the letters of the best answers in the blanks. Answer Key appears on page 137.

1. Lowell said:
   (a) "Some books should be digested"
   (b) "Books are the treasured wealth of the world"
   (c) "Few men learn the highest use of books"
   (d) "A good book is the precious life-blood of a master-spirit"   _____

2. The man who attributes to curiosity most of the important scientific contributions is:

   (a) Sir Isaac Newton   (c) Abraham Flexner
   (b) Galileo   (d) Albert Einstein   _____

3. This chapter tries to tell the reader, mainly:

   (a) how to read   (c) where and what to read
   (b) why to read   (d) all of these   _____

4. This chapter suggests you read to:
   (a) experience and converse
   (b) face the future and forget past history
   (c) develop curiosity and factual knowledge
   (d) none of these   _____

Match the following. Not all the items in the left-hand column can be matched; none is used twice.

(a) Cather	5. *Awakening* _____
(b) Wright	6. *Ethan Frome* _____
(c) Porter	7. *1984* _____
(d) Wharton	8. *My Antonia* _____
(e) Welty	9. *The Grapes of*
(f) Chopin	*Wrath* _____
(g) Steinbeck	10. *Flowering Judas* _____
(h) Huxley	
(i) Orwell	
(j) Jefferson	
(k) Locke	

Write the letters of the best answers in the blanks. Answer Key appears on page 137.

1. All readers are critics who evaluate literature in the light of:
   (a) their own taste
   (b) customary standards
   (c) both of these
   (d) neither of these   _____

2. As a critical reader you will begin to see that:
   (a) most critics are usually right
   (b) authors are humans, too
   (c) neither of these mentioned
   (d) both *a* and *b*   _____

3. According to this chapter, an actor must read a Shakespearean play until:
   (a) the groupings of the words come naturally
   (b) the pronunciation of the words comes naturally
   (c) the enunciation of the words comes naturally
   (d) none of these   _____

4. Good readers are not only critics, they are also:
   (a) creators
   (b) authors
   (c) playwrights
   (d) none of these   _____

5. Creative and critical reading are the supreme test of a skillful reader because they:
   (a) include every other reading skill
   (b) make use of past experiences in life and books
   (c) require an active and inquiring mind
   (d) all of these   _____

6. Readers can share in Shakespeare's superb imagination when they:
   (a) let their own imaginations grasp the play
   (b) read the play in the magnificent first folio edition
   (c) read the great critics on Shakespeare
   (d) all of these   _____

7. Being a critic means:
   (a) condemning slowly (praising with faint damns)
   (b) approving thoughtfully (damning with faint praise)
   (c) examining carefully
   (d) none of these   _____

8-10. (Choose the three best answers.) The duties of a critic, according to this chapter, are:
   (a) reviewing the best books available
   (b) finding exceptions to author's point of view
   (c) establishing a reasonably broad cultural background
   (d) reading Willa Cather's "Neighbor Rosicky"
   (e) upholding democratic standards of taste established by custom _____
   (f) checking generalizations against facts   _____
   (g) following the methods of John Ruskin and Matthew Arnold _____

Write the letters of the best answers in the blanks. Answer Key appears on page 137.

1. Many students object to analyzing a poem or story because:
   (a) the instrument of dissection is the mind
   (b) the authorship of a great work of literature is destroyed
   (c) a cold-blooded dissection destroys the beauty
   (d) it minimizes the liveliness of the work   _____

2. To understand and appreciate a book, a reader must:
   (a) know what the parts are
   (b) know the relationship of the parts
   (c) know what unites the parts
   (d) all of these   _____

3. When you strip the plot to its barest essentials, you should see:
   (a) its skeleton   (c) the essence of its parts
   (b) its good and bad parts   (d) none of these   _____

4. When you go to a play you will notice that:
   (a) each act is a play in itself
   (b) the whole is divided into three parts
   (c) the actors' parts are integrated into the whole
   (d) all of these   _____

Match the following. Not all the items in the left-hand column can be matched; none is used twice.

(a) moves toward a goal	5. Willy Loman	_____
(b) Emily Dickinson	6. X-ray	_____
(c) destroys beauty of organism	7. remark on dissecting insects	_____
	8. a very poor book	_____
(d) Alexander Pope	9. a very good book	_____
(e) *Gone with the Wind*	10. girl meets boy theme	_____
(f) like an amoeba		
(g) determines arrangement of parts		
(h) top of head blown off		
(i) *Macbeth*		
(j) paramecium		
(k) fall from high estate		

Write the letters of the best answers in the blanks. Answer Key appears on page 137.

1. The remarks of "people who know" carry authority because:
   (a) they have had wide and long experience
   (b) they have many influential friends
   (c) they observe sympathetically
   (d) all of these _____

2. You may infer that standards of judgment should represent:
   (a) the standards of custom
   (b) authoritative standards
   (c) the ideal toward which the performer strives
   (d) all of these _____

3. A standard of judgment mentioned in this chapter is:
   (a) legitimacy   (c) legality
   (b) legibility   (d) lexicography _____

4. Characteristics of a book which must *not* hinder reading are:
   (a) type size   (c) color of page and print
   (b) size of margins   (d) all of these _____

5. When we read for knowledge it is sufficient if the author imparts information:
   (a) quickly   (c) smoothly
   (b) clearly   (d) all of these _____

6. In a novel, the manner of expression must be:
   (a) mature, clear, and symbolic
   (b) appropriate, mature, and sensitive
   (c) clear, mature, and appropriate
   (d) all of these _____

7. The quotation about all words tending toward a pre-established design was by:
   (a) Edgar Lee Masters   (c) Edgar Allan Poe
   (b) Edgar Rice Burroughs   (d) Edward Guest _____

8. Most of the important standards of fiction are concerned with the effect of:
   (a) enrichment of life   (c) illuminating symbols
   (b) historical truth   (d) uplifting standards _____

9. A reader must constantly ask if the author has provided:
   (a) a plausible plot and true-to-life characters
   (b) a real feeling of liveliness
   (c) suitable standards of design
   (d) subject not mentioned _____

10. A work of fiction is as good or bad as:
    (a) the critics judge it   (c) you judge it
    (b) the author judges it   (d) subject not mentioned _____

Write the letters of the best answers in the blanks. Answer Key appears on page 137.

1. Emerson said that to read well one must be braced by:
   (a) spirit and body
   (b) joy and wisdom
   (c) labor and invention
   (d) none of these _____

2. A great work of literature should be read the first time for:
   (a) a careful analysis
   (b) subtle details of plot
   (c) fine points of characterization
   (d) sheer enjoyment _____

3. Great literature is often:
   (a) an original communication
   (b) a long and lively book
   (c) philosophical in nature
   (d) all of these _____

4. Great literature requires the reader to:
   (a) meditate
   (b) brood
   (c) reread
   (d) all of these _____

Match the following. Not all the items in the left-hand column can be matched; none is used twice.

(a) inspired writing
(b) *Huckleberry Finn*
(c) Mark Twain
(d) *Treasure Island*
(e) *Perpetual Books*
(f) great literature should inspire
(g) *American Scholar*
(h) *Sesame and Lilies*
(i) bring an active mind to reading
(j) Will Rogers
(k) *American Writer*
(l) a book perpetuates a truth an author has found

5. written by Ruskin _____
6. written by Emerson _____
7. "A great book is something everyone recommends and no one reads." _____
8. Emerson emphasized _____
9. Ruskin emphasized _____
10. classic American novel _____

Write the letters of the best answers in the blanks. Answer Key appears on page 137.

1. What test does the author use to define great authors?
    (a) the consensus of critics   (c) both *a* and *b*
    (b) rereading them frequently   (d) neither *a* nor *b*   _____

2. A book mentioned as not holding up to the test of rereading was:
    (a) *The Human Comedy*   (c) *For Whom the Bell Tolls*
    (b) *Of Time and the River*   (d) none of these   _____

3. Two works were mentioned which seem new to the author each time they are reread. They are *Huck Finn* and
    (a) Emerson's essays   (c) Thoreau's *Walden*
    (b) Poe's stories   (d) Hawthorne's *The Scarlet Letter*   _____

4. Why are there fresh things to be discovered in rereading?
    (a) one's life changes   (c) new biographies appear
    (b) the eras change   (d) both *a* and *b*   _____

5. Freud's theories of infant sexuality used analytical symbols such as:
    (a) the id   (c) the libido
    (b) the ego   (d) all of these mentioned   _____

6. In addition to the Freudian approach, another critical approach was mentioned. The approach was:
    (a) feminist   (c) minimalist
    (b) post-constructionist   (d) none of these   _____

7. A trend in short stories is away from innovation toward new ways of depicting
    (a) character   (c) setting
    (b) plot   (d) atmosphere   _____

8. The title of the book used to illustrate a change over four decades is:
    (a) *Huck Finn*   (c) *The Catcher in the Rye*
    (b) *Walden*   (d) *Catch-22*   _____

9. Rereading allows you to see how much has changed in:
    (a) your taste   (c) contemporary literature
    (b) the spirit of the times   (d) both *a* and *b*   _____

10. In the Twain quotation, how old is his father?
    (a) subject not mentioned   (c) 55
    (b) 45   (d) 65   _____

Write the letters of the best answers in the blanks. Answer Key appears on page 137.

1. Instead of a handle the $700 toilet has a:
   - (a) gold chain
   - (b) silver lever
   - (c) flush actuator
   - (d) door lever
   _____

2. The "nym" part of "bumpernym" means:
   - (a) car
   - (b) word
   - (c) name
   - (d) humor
   _____

3. Twain wrote of something that "swept on motionless wing." It was a:
   - (a) large bird
   - (b) early airplane
   - (c) low-flying cloud
   - (d) esophagus
   _____

4. "Related social-expression merchandise" means:
   - (a) T-shirts
   - (b) coffee mugs
   - (c) both of these
   - (d) subject not explained
   _____

5. The ram in the Twain story headed toward Jim's grandfather at:
   - (a) 20 mph
   - (b) 30 mph
   - (c) 40 mph
   - (d) speed not mentioned
   _____

6. Eventually the ram in the Twain story:
   - (a) butted the man
   - (b) was distracted
   - (c) stopped in his tracks
   - (d) tale does not explain
   _____

7. The woman in the "worst novel" example was:
   - (a) Julia
   - (b) Helen
   - (c) Lynn
   - (d) none of these
   _____

8. In the one-liner about cats, Twain complained of their:
   - (a) fighting noise
   - (b) grammar
   - (c) screeching
   - (d) aloofness
   _____

9. A reversal of expectations is one definition of:
   - (a) humor
   - (b) word hoarding
   - (c) substituting language
   - (d) zapping the reader
   _____

10. The Bulwer-Lytton contest was sponsored by:
    - (a) San Diego State University
    - (b) Buffalo State University
    - (c) San Jose State University
    - (d) Wright State University
    _____

Write the letters of the best answers in the blanks. Answer Key appears on page 137.

1. The two chief sources for reviews of contemporary books are:
   (a) major magazines and the Sunday edition of *The New York Times*
   (b) *The Book Review Digest* and *The Chicago Tribune*
   (c) Great Books Foundation and Classics Club
   (d) none of these _____

2. Most book critics:
   (a) get paid to praise
   (b) praise the majority of books they review
   (c) cannot be independent of the publisher who pays them
   (d) none of these _____

3. In addition to the Bible, the works of the following have had the greatest influence on our time:
   (a) Darwin, Marx, Newton   (c) Darwin, Newton, Freud
   (b) Marx, Newton, Einstein   (d) Freud, Darwin, Marx _____

4. The mark of well-educated persons is their familiarity with:
   (a) cultured friends   (c) the ideas in popular books
   (b) world problems and   (d) none of these
   conditions _____

5. *The Book Review Digest*
   (a) is published every ten years
   (b) provides all critical opinion on a book
   (c) both of these
   (d) neither of these _____

6. *Good Reading* provides:
   (a) a test of "whodunits"   (c) reading for English teachers
   (b) the Great Books Foundation (d) none of these
   test _____

7. This chapter implies that the Great Books Foundation wants to:
   (a) present exciting reading material
   (b) make profits by educating the masses
   (c) stimulate, more than anything else, people's thinking
   (d) none of these _____

8. A book becomes great by its:
   (a) popularity with critics
   (b) conversational value among the best people
   (c) best-seller status
   (d) none of these _____

9. The number of books published forces the reader to:
   (a) read efficiently   (c) select only the best books
   (b) read more frequently   (d) read as many reviews as
                                     possible _____

10. This chapter implies that the ultimate purpose of this book is to:
    (a) teach efficient reading
    (b) create a strong desire to read
    (c) encourage reading more good books
    (d) present all the important aspects of reading _____

Answer Keys

Application Exercise

Chapter 1 (page 6)

1. N, X, B
2. X, B, N
3. N, X, B

Vocabulary in Context I *(page 20)*

In Chapter 1 the definition of "aroused" is 4, "provoked"; therefore, you write 4 in the first blank.

Chapter 1	Chapter 3	Chapter 4
1. 4	1. 6	1. 2
2. 6	2. 4	2. 5
3. 1	3. 11	3. 8
4. 8	4. 8	4. 7
5. 3	5. 10	5. 6
6. 5	6. 5	6. 3
7. 2	7. 9	7. 9
8. 7	8. 7	8. 4
	9. 1	9. 1
	10. 3	
	11. 2	

Vocabulary in Context II *(page 47)*

Chapter 5	Chapter 6	Chapter 8
1. 5	1. 4	1. 6
2. 10	2. 6	2. 4
3. 9	3. 1	3. 5
4. 1	4. 2	4. 2
5. 6	5. 3	5. 3
6. 4	6. 5	6. 1
7. 2		
8. 8		
9. 3		
10. 7		

Application Exercises

Chapter 11 (page 51)

1. 1
2. 8
3. 4
4. 6
5. 3
6. 5
7. 7
8. 2

Chapter 12 (page 56)

1. bungling	5. involve	9. expose
2. fight	6. duty	10. succession
3. extinct	7. snag	11. terminal
4. incite	8. phase	12. drudgery

Vocabulary in Context III *(page 103)*

Chapters 16 and 19

1. 7
2. 2
3. 6
4. 4
5. 9
6. 3
7. 10
8. 5
9. 8
10. 1

Chapter 20

1. 5
2. 1
3. 6
4. 2
5. 7
6. 8
7. 4
8. 3

Chapter 21

1. 3
2. 1
3. 7
4. 5
5. 4
6. 8
7. 9
8. 2
9. 6

Chapters 22 and 23

1. 11
2. 3
3. 5
4. 9
5. 2
6. 4
7. 1
8. 10
9. 6
10. 8
11. 7

Application Exercise

Chapter 24 (page 108)

True statements are 4, 9, 13, 17, 25, 29, 32, 40, 41, 44.

Comprehension Checks

Chapter 1	Chapter 2	Chapter 3	Chapter 4
1. b	1. d	1. b	1. c
2. c	2. c	2. a	2. a
3. d	3. d	3. c	3. a
4. c	4. c	4. c	4. c
5. d	5. b	5. d	5. d
6. a	6. c	6. c	6. c
7. a	7. b	7. a	7. c
8. a	8. d	8. b	8. a
9. d	9. b	9. d	9. c
10. d	10. a	10. c	10. d

Chapter 5	Chapter 6	Chapter 7	Chapter 8
1. d	1. c	1. d	1. a
2. c	2. c	2. a	2. a
3. c	3. c	3. a	3. c
4. a	4. b	4. c	4. a
5. b	5. b	5. d	5. c
6. d	6. d	6. a	6. c
7. d	7. d	7. c	7. c
8. c	8. a	8. b	8. b
9. c	9. c	9. d	9. d
10. c	10. c	10. d	10. d

Chapter 9	Chapter 10	Chapter 11	Chapter 12
1. d	1. d	1. e	1. d
2. a	2. a	2. d	2. d
3. b	3. b	3. a	3. a
4. a	4. c	4. b	4. b
5. d	5. a	5. g	5. a
6. a	6. a	6. h	6. c
7. d	7. d	7. f	7. b
8. c	8. c	8. i	8. d
9. b	9. a	9. j	9. d
10. a	10. d	10. k	10. c

Chapter 13	Chapter 14	Chapter 15	Chapter 16
1. d	1. d	1. m	1. d
2. d	2. c	2. n	2. c
3. a	3. a	3. g	3. d
4. d	4. a	4. r	4. d
5. c	5. c	5. y	5. d
6. a	6. a	6. s	6. d
7. a	7. c	7. x	7. d
8. a	8. b	8. w	8. b
9. d	9. c	9. q	9. c
10. d	10. d	10. f	10. b

Chapter 17	Chapter 18	Chapter 19	Chapter 20
1. c	1. c	1. c	1. a
2. c	2. b	2. d	2. c
3. b	3. a	3. c	3. b
4. c	4. a	4. d	4. d
5. f	5. d	5. k	5. b
6. d	6. c	6. g	6. c
7. i	7. a	7. d	7. c
8. a	8. b	8. f	8. a
9. g	9. c	9. a	9. a
10. c	10. f	10. e	10. c

Chapter 21	Chapter 22	Chapter 23	Chapter 24
1. c	1. b	1. c	1. a
2. d	2. b	2. c	2. d
3. a	3. c	3. d	3. d
4. d	4. d	4. d	4. d
5. h	5. d	5. c	5. d
6. g	6. a	6. d	6. d
7. c	7. a	7. a	7. c
8. i	8. c	8. b	8. d
9. l	9. d	9. a	9. c
10. b	10. a	10. c	10. c

Graph of Progress in Rate and Comprehension

Directions: Record your rate (on the chart) and your comprehension (in the square above the chart) after you have read each chapter.

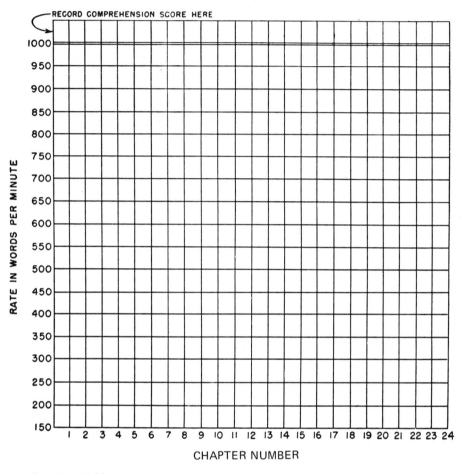

Time-Rate Table

Time in minutes and seconds converted to rate in words per minute.

Time	Rate	Time	Rate	Time	Rate	Time	Rate	Time	Rate
1:00	1000	2:00	500	3:00	333	4:00	250	5:00	200
1:05	933	2:05	481	3:05	324	4:05	245	5:05	197
1:10	857	2:10	461	3:10	316	4:10	240	5:10	194
1:15	800	2:15	445	3:15	308	4:15	235	5:15	192
1:20	752	2:20	429	3:20	299	4:20	230	5:20	188
1:25	704	2:25	415	3:25	290	4:25	225	5:25	184
1:30	666	2:30	400	3:30	281	4:30	221	5:30	180
1:35	633	2:35	384	3:35	276	4:35	218	5:35	178
1:40	602	2:40	376	3:40	271	4:40	215	5:40	176
1:45	571	2:45	364	3:45	266	4:45	211	5:45	172
1:50	546	2:50	353	3:50	260	4:50	208	5:50	170
1:55	524	2:55	343	3:55	255	4:55	204	5:55	168